WHO

DID IT?

WHO DID IT?

A BIBLE QUIZ CHALLENGE
FOR KIDS

ELIJAH ADKINS

BARBOUR **kidz**
A Division of Barbour Publishing

Published by Barbour Publishing, Inc., 1810 Barbour Drive, Uhrichsville, Ohio 44683, www.barbourbooks.com

Our mission is to inspire the world with the life-changing message of the Bible.

Member of the
Evangelical Christian
Publishers Association

Printed in the United States of America.

002426 0225 BP

WHO DID IT?

- *built the ark*
- *killed Goliath*
- *gave birth to Jesus*
- *saw the writing on the wall*
- *multiplied a widow's cooking oil*

You'll find these questions—and 395 others just like them—inside this book. Show what you know about Bible characters and the things they did with this fun and fascinating quiz.

Covering the whole of scripture, from Genesis to Revelation, *Who Did It?* will test your memory of dozens of Bible stories. Questions are organized into four categories:

- Too Easy!
- A Little Tougher
- Hard as Rock
- We Hope You're a Good Guesser

Whether or not you can answer every question, you'll love learning more about God's Word. And that's the most important thing of all!

NOTE:

The spelling of personal names and places match the translations cited in the Answer Key, which begins on page 111.

TOO EASY!

1. He was the first to walk on water:
   a) Abraham
   b) Adam
   c) Jesus
   d) Paul

2. She was everyone's mother:

   __ __ __

3. True or False: Timothy spent a night with the lions.

4. His coat was very colorful:

   __ __ __ __ __ __

5. He refused to let God's people go:
- a) King Saul
- b) Pharaoh
- c) Ezekiel
- d) Moses

6. True or False: Noah built the ark.

7. She saved the Jews from Haman's evil plan:
- a) Esther
- b) Rebekah
- c) Miriam
- d) Mary

8. God pointed out this man's righteousness to Satan: ___ ___ ___

9. He used a fleece to make sure God was calling him:
   a) Titus
   b) Gideon
   c) Joab
   d) Darius the Mede

10. True or False: Jonathan was Jesus' earthly "dad."

11. He killed Goliath:

   — — — — —

12. True or False: Ishmael was called the father of many nations.

13. He killed his own brother in a field:
   a) Adam
   b) Cain
   c) Methuselah
   d) Nehemiah

14. True or False: Pilate washed his hands
to say he was innocent of Jesus' death.

15. One of these men mocked Jesus;
the other changed his mind just in time:
   a) the two witnesses
   b) the thieves hanging on crosses
   c) Paul and Silas
   d) David and Jonathan

16. He planted the Garden of Eden:

— — —

17. He was the wisest king:
   a) Ahab
   b) Nebuchadnezzar
   c) Solomon
   d) Herod

18. True or False: King Saul told Delilah his secret.

19. His book describes his vision of a bone-filled valley:

— — — — — — —

20. He was told to go to Nineveh:
   a) Jonah
   b) Jonathan
   c) John
   d) Jeroboam

21. He went to heaven in a whirlwind:

— — — — — —

22. True or False: Judas betrayed Jesus.

23. He was short. . .but determined to see Jesus:
  a) Nicodemus
  b) Andrew
  c) Zaccheus
  d) Bartholomew

24. He led his troops to march around Jericho:

— — — — — —

25. True or False: Thomas was a doubting disciple.

26. He brought life into the world:
   a) Cain
   b) Paul
   c) Jesus Christ
   d) Adam

27. This child was found in a basket floating in the river:
   a) Job
   b) Paul
   c) Moses
   d) Darius the Mede

28. True or False: Abigail was bathing when David saw her.

29. He hid with his wife after eating forbidden fruit:

— — — —

30. He was released instead of Jesus:
   a) Barabbas
   b) Peter
   c) Pilate
   d) James

31. This animal talked to a man named Balaam:

— — — — — —

32. True or False: Noah saw a rainbow, the sign of God's promise.

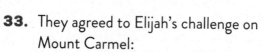

33. They agreed to Elijah's challenge on Mount Carmel:
   a) the Philistines
   b) prophets of Baal
   c) the twelve disciples
   d) the Gibeonites

34. She helped out the Israelite spies:

— — — — —

35. True or False: Peter wrote the book of Revelation.

36. He married Ruth:
   a) the apostle Paul
   b) Nehemiah
   c) Joel
   d) Boaz

37. True or False: Saul was blinded on the road to Rome.

38. She gave birth to Jesus:

— — — —

39. This person was almost Abraham's sacrifice:
   a) his wife Sarah
   a) his servant Eliezer
   b) his nephew Lot
   c) his son Isaac

40. They were in a field when an angel announced Jesus' birth:

— — — — — — — — — —

41. They drove 2,000 pigs to a watery death:

    a) angels
    b) Pharisees
    c) demons
    d) Gentiles

42. He was the most famous person baptized by John:

    — — — — —

43. True or False: The people of Jericho repented when they heard Jonah's message.

44. He tried to kill young David:

    a) Jonathan
    b) King Saul
    c) Daniel
    d) Samuel

45. Paul and Silas sang in this surprising

place: __ __ __ __ __ __

46. He inspired Judas to betray Jesus:
a) Nicodemus
b) Satan
c) Andrew
d) Baal

47. They safely crossed the Red Sea on dry
ground:
a) the Egyptians
b) the Ammonites
c) the Babylonians
d) the Israelites

48. True or False: In Jesus' parable,
a Samaritan helped an injured traveler.

49. They came from the east, following a star, to see baby Jesus:

— — — —   — — —

50. Three of them came to Job when they heard about his suffering:
   a) angels
   b) daughters
   c) friends
   d) demons

51. True or False: The tentmakers of Egypt were able to imitate a few of Moses' miracles.

52. This apostle denied Jesus three times:

— — — — —

53. True or False: Solomon wrote most of the Proverbs.

54. Aaron was chosen to speak for this man, his famous brother:

__ __ __ __ __

55. He destroyed the wicked cities of Sodom and Gomorrah:
   a) Satan
   b) Lot
   c) the Lord
   d) Abraham

56. True or False: Samson died when he toppled a building on himself and his enemies.

57. She gave birth to John the Baptist:

__ __ __ __ __ __ __ __ __

58. He agreed to work seven years to marry Rachel:
a) Jacob
b) Abimelech
c) Samson
d) Aquila

59. The queen of this land traveled to test Solomon's wisdom:

__ __ __ __ __

60. They and the scribes didn't practice what they preached—and Jesus called them out.
a) Jews
b) Gentiles
c) Pharisees
d) Romans

61. True or False: Jesus once wore a crown of thorns.

62. He prayed while inside a fish's belly:
a) Amos
b) Peter
c) Jonah
d) Moses

63. This king saw a fourth man in the fire:

__ __ __ __ __ __ __ __ __

__ __ __ __ __ __

64. True or False: Something like scales once fell from John's eyes.

65. She was Cain and Abel's mom:
  a) Esther
  b) Eve
  c) Michal
  d) Jochebed

66. This king was injured, so he asked another man to finish him off:

__ __ __ __

67. True or False: When Moses died, David replaced him as the man to lead the Israelites.

68. In Jesus' parable, this man was forgiven by God while the Pharisee wasn't:
  a) a prophet
  b) a Samaritan
  c) a tax collector
  d) a rich man

69. He was an Old Testament prophet:
   a) Ezekiel
   b) Jesus
   c) Peter
   d) Zacchaeus

70. He was a man after God's own heart.
   a) Abraham
   b) David
   c) Saul
   d) Micah

71. This prophet prayed, and God brought fire down from heaven:

   __ __ __ __ __ __

72. True or False: Cain fell into a deep sleep, and God took one of his ribs to make a woman.

73. He prayed three times each day as he always had, disobeying the king's command:
   a) Nehemiah
   b) Paul
   c) Daniel
   d) Elijah

74. He saw a burning bush that never burned up: __ __ __ __ __

75. He rose from the grave on the third day:
   a) Solomon
   b) Jesus Christ
   c) Paul
   d) Jonah

76. True or False: Paul had a "thorn in the flesh."

77. His sacrifice pleased God more than his brother's did: ___ ___ ___ ___

78. He walked with God and suddenly vanished because God "took" him:
a) Moses
b) Enoch
c) Noah
d) Epaphroditus

79. True or False: Seth didn't sin with his lips, even when he lost everything.

80. This Jewish woman was chosen by the king of Persia to become his new queen:.

___ ___ ___ ___ ___ ___

81. He told the woman at the well that she'd had five husbands:
a) Jesus Christ
b) Peter
c) Elijah
d) John the Baptist

82. He wrestled with God:

__ __ __ __ __

83. This man married Rebekah:
a) Adam
b) Malachi
c) Esau
d) Isaac

84. True or False: A man and a woman came to Solomon with an argument over a baby.

85. He turned over tables in the temple:

___ ___ ___ ___ ___

86. True or False: The Holy Spirit came to earth on the day of Pentecost.

87. He sent an east wind to part the Red Sea:
  a) the Lord
  b) Moses
  c) Elijah
  d) Gabriel

88. He fell like lightning from heaven:

___ ___ ___ ___ ___

89. He ordered that all newborn boys be thrown into the river:

— — — — — — —

90. True or False: God gave names to the animals.

91. He killed all the boys in Bethlehem who were two years old and younger:
   a) Noah
   b) King Herod
   c) Goliath
   d) Legion

92. True or False: The Pharisees tempted Jesus in the desert.

93. "The Helper" is another name for:
  a) Michael the archangel
  b) the Holy Spirit
  c) Samson
  d) King Josiah

94. This leader taxed the whole world at the time when Jesus was born:
  a) Caesar Augustus
  b) David
  c) Ahab
  d) King Og

95. He wrote down God's Law:

  — — — — —

96. True or False: The fool says that there is no God.

97. This prophet got mad when a city repented:
   a) Elijah
   b) Moses
   c) Jonah
   d) John the Baptist

98. He refused to turn rocks into bread:

— — — — —

99. God parted the Red Sea while this man held his hand over it:
   a) Hezekiah
   b) Moses
   c) Pharaoh
   d) Luke

100. True or False: God gave His Son to save the world.

A LITTLE
TOUGHER

1. His wife looked back and became a pillar of salt: ___ ___ ___

2. He wrote the book of Romans:
   a) King David
   b) Peter
   c) Jesus Christ
   d) Paul

3. True or False: Saul was Israel's first king.

4. He was a tax collector when Jesus called him:

   ___ ___ ___ ___ ___ ___ ___

5. This disciple was the second (and last) person to walk on water:
   a) Andrew
   b) Peter
   c) John
   d) Judas

6. She was Jacob's favorite wife:

__ __ __ __ __ __

7. True or False: Moses saw an Assyrian beating up a Hebrew.

8. True or False: Jesus called James and John the "sons of sunshine."

9. He was a real-life mummy, brought back to life by Jesus:

__ __ __ __ __ __ __

10. His Gospel begins with the same three words as Genesis 1, "In the beginning."
a) Matthew
b) Mark
c) Luke
d) John

11. She told the suffering Job to curse God:
a) his wife
b) his daughter
c) his niece
d) his sister

12. True or False: Joshua was the son of a man called Nun.

13. He touched the ark of God and died:

— — — — —

14. True or False: Jesus Christ created everything.

15. A wooden gallows was built for the purpose of hanging him.
   a) John
   b) Mordecai
   c) King Josiah
   d) Eutychus

16. He was Joseph's Egyptian master:

— — — — — — — —

17. She was Ishmael's mom:
   a) Mary
   b) Martha
   c) Phoebe
   d) Hagar

18. True or False: The people of Babylon gave Aaron gold to make a golden calf idol.

19. His tribe made up the priests of Israel:

   — — — —

20. He had a hot oven, and he made it even hotter:
   a) Absalom
   b) Nebuchadnezzar
   c) Abednego
   d) John Mark

21. He prophesied that a virgin would give birth:

— — — — — —

22. True or False: King Agrippa said Jesus almost persuaded him to become a Christian.

23. This woman scared the prophet Elijah:
   a) Abigail
   b) Jezebel
   c) Maacah
   d) Joanna

24. Two of them stood in Jesus' empty tomb:

— — — — — —

25. When God told this woman she'd have a child, she couldn't help but chuckle:
   a) Sarah
   b) Bernice
   c) Zipporah
   d) Mary

26. True or False: Elisha got the Ten Commandments on tablets of stone directly from God.

27. This woman stayed with Naomi rather than returning to her own family:

   __ __ __ __

28. He appeared to Solomon in a dream at Gibeon:
   a) Samuel
   b) Gabriel
   c) the LORD
   d) Shadrach

29. True or False: Saul was David's closest friend.

30. A man named Ananias helped this new Christian heal from blindness:

__ __ __ __

31. True or False: King Josiah asked a witch for help.

32. True or False: Abraham's servant searched for a wife for his master's son.

33. This king, one of several with this name, was criticized by John the Baptist:

— — — — —

34. He was cast into a deep, muddy well for his prophecies:
   a) Moses
   b) Agabus
   c) Amos
   d) Jeremiah

35. He baptized a person, and then the Spirit took him far away:
   a) Jesus Christ
   b) Philip
   c) Solomon
   d) Ezekiel

36. True or False: The prodigal son's older brother ran out to meet him when he returned.

37. This Egyptian king had a dream about cows coming out of the Nile River:

＿ ＿ ＿ ＿ ＿ ＿ ＿

38. He chose five smooth stones over a set of armor:
   a) Stephen
   b) Joshua
   c) David
   d) Adam

39. True or False: The prophet Habakkuk accused King David of a terrible sin.

40. He dreamed of a ladder reaching up to heaven: ＿ ＿ ＿ ＿ ＿

41. He escaped from a violent crowd near the edge of a cliff:
a) Paul
b) Joshua
c) Jesus
d) Noah

42. True or False: Sarah was once called Savannah.

43. This beautiful queen was Mordecai's cousin:

— — — — — —

44. This Gospel writer was also a doctor:
a) Matthew
b) Mark
c) Luke
d) John

45. True or False: Peter preached on the day of Pentecost, when the Holy Spirit came to earth.

46. He explained some spooky writing on the wall of a king's palace:

__ __ __ __ __ __

47. This man, along with Joshua, believed the Israelites should enter the Promised Land:
   a) Methuselah
   b) Caleb
   c) Isaiah
   d) John Mark

48. True or False: Judas Iscariot asked Pontius Pilate for Jesus' body.

49. This man called his beautiful wife his sister because he was afraid someone would kill him to get her:

— — — — — — —

50. True or False: Jude wrote the book of 1 Timothy.

51. He asked Elijah for a "double portion" of his spirit:

— — — — — —

52. After working seven years for Rachel, Jacob was tricked into marrying *this* woman instead:
  a) Eve
  b) Leah
  c) Deborah
  d) Mary Magdalene

53. True or False: Moses built a fancy house in the Promised Land.

54. He was only eight when he became king of Jerusalem:

— — — — — —

55. He was the oldest man in the Bible:
   a) Adam
   b) Noah
   c) Methuselah
   d) Matthew

56. He was cursed by God to be a wanderer:

— — — —

57. True or False: King Herod killed John the Baptist.

58. This woman was an old, widowed prophetess who stayed in the temple:
a) Mary Magdalene
b) Anna
c) Sapphira
d) Joanna

59. This prophet got on a ship headed to Tarshish:

— — — — —

60. True or False: Solomon wrote a love song.

61. His brothers covered his coat in goat's blood to fool their dad:

__ __ __ __ __ __

62. This New Testament prophet ate a book in a vision:
   a) Agabus
   b) Philip
   c) John
   d) Jesus Christ

63. He smashed an altar of Baal at night:

__ __ __ __ __ __

64. He was a Christ-like mystery man with no known mom or dad:
   a) Melchizedek
   b) Judah
   c) Aaron
   d) Darius the Mede

65. True or False: Abner was David's dad.

66. He challenged the army of Israel to provide one man to fight him:

— — — — — — —

67. He came to Jesus at night and admitted Jesus had come from God:
   a) Nathanael
   b) Nicodemus
   c) Nathan
   d) Naaman

68. This wicked king married Jezebel:

— — — —

69. True or False: Esther was Israel's only
female judge.

70. Her price is far above rubies:
   a) a brawling woman
   b) a virtuous woman
   c) a "strange" woman
   d) a fair woman

71. He stooped down and drew in the dust
in response to others' questions:

— — — — —

72. True or False: Young Samuel heard
God's voice at night but didn't know it
was Him.

73. He talked with God face to face:

— — — — —

74. He was bitten by a snake that slithered out of a fire:
   a) Luke
   b) Jesus Christ
   c) Herod Agrippa
   d) Paul

75. Paul planted the gospel seed, Apollos watered it, but who caused it to grow?

— — —

76. His book describes how Jerusalem's wall was rebuilt:
   a) Joel
   b) Nehemiah
   c) Jeremiah
   d) Nahum

77. True or False: King Zedekiah got an extra fifteen years of life.

78. His name was changed to Israel:

— — — — —

79. He didn't believe an angel, so he lost his ability to speak for a while:
   a) Zacchaeus
   b) Zacharias
   c) John the Baptist
   d) Philip the Evangelist

80. Ten of them came to Jesus for healing:

— — — — — —

81. He heard God speak from a whirlwind:
 a) Adam
 b) King Saul
 c) Job
 d) Peter

82. True or False: The elders of Egypt asked Samuel for a king.

83. This prophet broke all Ten Commandments—literally:

— — — — —

84. He was a special servant of God—a Nazarite—from birth:
 a) Eli
 b) Aaron
 c) Samson
 d) Zacharias

85. True or False: The apostle Paul spent ten years under house arrest.

86. King David lost him because of his sin with Bathsheba:
   a) his nephew
   b) his father
   c) his child
   d) his brother

87. Caiaphas held this job during Jesus' trial:

   __ __ __ __

   __ __ __ __ __ __

88. A cheerful one of these is loved by God:
   a) preacher
   b) elder
   c) giver
   d) helper

89. True or False: Abraham's face shone after talking with God.

90. They tricked Herod by taking a different road home:

— — — —

— — —

91. He was protected by God with a mark:
a) Cain
b) Adam
c) Jacob
d) Paul

92. True or False: Amos refused to bow to Nebuchadnezzar's golden statue.

93. This Gospel writer started off by listing Jesus' ancestors right away:

__ __ __ __ __ __ __

94. They cared for Jesus after He was tempted:
  a) His disciples
  b) the Sadducees
  c) angels
  d) the kings of the earth

95. True or False: Bathsheba gave birth to Solomon.

96. He provided wine for a wedding in Cana: __ __ __ __ __

97. They ate manna in the wilderness:
   a) Egyptians
   b) Philistines
   c) Israelites
   d) the twelve disciples

98. True or False: King Herod had 700 wives.

99. He brought death into the world:

   __ __ __ __

100. He wanted to kill every Jewish person in Persia: __ __ __ __ __

HARD AS
ROCK

1. He sinned by counting the people of Israel:
   a) Mephibosheth
   b) Daniel
   c) David
   d) Hosea

2. He turned a donkey's jawbone into a weapon:

— — — — — —

3. True or False: Paul saw all kinds of animals coming down on a sheet from heaven.

4. This religious group didn't believe in the resurrection:
   a) Essenes
   b) Pharisees
   c) Sadducees
   d) Zealots

5. He played a hairy trick on his dad:

__ __ __ __ __

6. This man was a runaway slave who met the apostle Paul:
   a) Philip
   b) James
   c) Onesimus
   d) Mark

7. He was sitting under a fig tree when Jesus first saw him:
   a) Nathanael
   b) Mordecai
   c) Herod
   d) Nicodemus

8. He fell off a chair and broke his neck after receiving bad news:

__ __ __

9. He lost an ear to Peter's sword:
   a) Mark
   b) Malchus
   c) Malachi
   d) Meshach

10. True or False: Achan sinned by taking an "accursed thing."

11. He died in battle because David arranged for it:

   __ __ __ __ __

12. True or False: Jeremiah described an angel touching his lips with a hot coal.

13. He accurately predicted a shipwreck:
   a) King Ahab
   b) Jonah
   c) Paul
   d) Philemon

14. He and Nadab burned "strange fire":

   __ __ __ __ __

15. True or false: James was Jesus' brother.

16. He was the first Christian who was stoned to death for his faith:
   a) Peter
   b) James
   c) Philip
   d) Stephen

17. He was a thieving disciple:

— — — — —

— — — — — — — —

18. True or False: Simon Peter helped carry Jesus' cross.

19. She led the Israelite ladies in song and dance after they escaped from slavery in Egypt:

— — — — — —

20. He literally flew in a hurry to give Daniel a message:
a) Gabriel
b) Jehu
c) Shadrach
d) Legion

21. True or False: Naaman was told by a prophet to take a bath.

22. This Gospel writer deserted from Paul during a trip to Pamphylia:

— — — —

23. True or False: Peter and John healed a blind man by spitting on his eyes.

24. Philip chased down this person's chariot:
   a) an Ethiopian eunuch
   b) the queue of Sheba
   c) the widow of Nain
   d) Joseph of Arimathea

25. True or False: Noah's three daughters and their husbands boarded the ark with him.

26. True or False: At the Mount of Transfiguration, Moses and Joshua appeared with Jesus.

27. She watched baby Moses' basket in the river from a distance:
a) his mother
b) his sister
c) his aunt
d) his grandmother

28. She killed an enemy army commander with a tent peg: __ __ __ __

29. Not much was left of her after she fell from a great height:
a) Priscilla
b) Ruth
c) Tamar
d) Jezebel

30. This daughter-in-law kissed Naomi goodbye: __ __ __ __ __

31. He asked why Nehemiah was so sad:
a) King Artaxerxes
b) Sanballat
c) Isaiah
d) Satan

32. His dead spirit was brought up by a witch at Endor:

__ __ __ __ __ __

33. This older brother had second thoughts about killing young Joseph:
   a) Benjamin
   b) Judah
   c) Reuben
   d) Jacob

34. He is the dragon, the "old snake" cast out of heaven in a vision in Revelation:

   __ __ __ __ __

35. She had a terrible dream about Jesus before His trial:
   a) Pilate's wife
   b) Herod's daughter
   c) Peter's mother-in-law
   d) Jesus' mother

36. True or False: The New Testament prophet Agabus tied a belt around his hands and feet.

37. True or False: Peter's name means "rock."

38. This judge caught 300 foxes, tied their tails together, and set them on fire to burn an enemy's fields:
a) Samson
b) Gideon
c) Ehud
d) Deborah

39. She gathered grain behind the workmen in a field:

__ __ __ __

40. True or False: The king of Moab died with a sword through the stomach.

41. He slept on a stony pillow one night:
   a) Jacob
   b) Jesus Christ
   c) Peter
   d) Abraham

42. This military leader was too scared to fight without Deborah:

   __ __ __ __ __

43. This king saw the writing on the wall:
   a) Nebuchadnezzar
   b) Belshazzar
   c) Hezekiah
   d) Darius the Mede

44. He was Moses' father-in-law from Midian:

   __ __ __ __ __ __ __

45. He killed the firstborn in Egypt:
   a) the angel of death
   b) the LORD
   c) Satan
   d) Moses

46. True or False: Hezekiah prayed for God to make the sundial, an ancient clock, run backward.

47. This pagan god's statue fell before God's ark and broke apart:

   __ __ __ __ __

48. The butler got his job back, and this man was hanged, just as their dreams had indicated:
   a) Pharaoh's baker
   b) Pharaoh's magician
   c) Potiphar
   d) Joseph

49. True or False: John wrote the book of Titus.

50. He promised God he would sacrifice whatever came out of his house to meet him:

  — — — — — — — —

51. This father fooled Jacob by giving his daughter Leah in marriage instead of Rachel:
   a) Esau
   b) Isaac
   c) Joseph
   d) Laban

52. True or False: David built God's temple.

53. This man's tribe is associated with a lion:

__ __ __ __ __

54. True or False: Noah got drunk after the flood.

55. He was picked to join the twelve disciples after Judas killed himself:

__ __ __ __ __ __ __

56. This man was shocked to see Joseph's silver cup in his sack of grain:
   a) Benjamin
   b) Judah
   c) Issachar
   d) Pharaoh

57. True or False: A demon-possessed servant girl shouted that Paul was a follower of God.

58. These fearsome enemies of Israel captured the ark of God:
a) the Romans
b) the Babylonians
c) the Philistines
d) the Egyptians

59. This king died in a chariot with an arrow stuck through a gap in his armor:

— — — —

60. True or False: The Assyrians' chariot wheels fell off at God's command.

61. He told Peter to pull a coin from a fish's mouth:
   a) Nicodemus
   b) Jarius
   c) Paul
   d) Jesus Christ

62. He married an unfaithful woman. . .under God's command:

   __ __ __ __ __

63. True or False: Samuel wanted to build God a temple.

64. This is how the author of the book of Ecclesiastes is described:
   a) the disciple whom Jesus loved
   b) the rich young ruler
   c) the Preacher
   d) the virtuous woman

65. In Revelation, he stood on the earth's sea and land:
   a) an angel
   b) God the Father
   c) Jesus Christ
   d) the beast

66. He didn't give God the glory, so he was eaten by worms:

   — — — — —

67. True or False: Paul survived a stoning.

68. He lied. . .and died on the spot:
   a) Nabal
   b) Judas Iscariot
   c) Ananias
   d) Pharaoh

69. This Old Testament prophet came back in the form of John the Baptist:

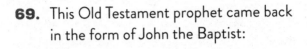

70. True or False: Absalom's death devastated King Solomon.

71. He caught a glimpse of God as the Lord walked by:
   a) Abraham
   b) Paul
   c) Simeon
   d) Moses

72. True or False: Shepherds brought gold, frankincense, and myrrh to Jesus.

◀ ▶
▼

73. This kingly priest met Abraham and blessed him:

— — — — — — —

— — — — —

74. The priest Eli thought she was drunk, but she was actually praying silently:
   a) Hannah
   b) Miriam
   c) Mary
   d) Hagar

75. His prayer mentions seaweed wrapped around his head: __ __ __ __ __

76. Bible prophets didn't make up their own message—they spoke whenever He moved them:
   a) God the Father
   b) God the Son
   c) God the Holy Spirit
   d) The Trinity

77. True or False: The Preacher in Ecclesiastes said, "All is vanity" (or "useless").

78. This Bible author was a cupbearer (someone who carried and tested wine) for the Persian king:

__ __ __ __ __ __ __ __

79. His blood cried to God from the ground:
a) Abel
b) Abimelech
c) Cain
d) Adam

80. True or False: Samson killed a lion and later took honey from its body.

81. He was sent away to an island called Patmos for his faith:
   a) James
   b) Jude
   c) John
   d) Jonah

82. She got water for the camels of Abraham's servant:

— — — — — — —

83. True or False: Joseph got attention he didn't like or want from his master's wife.

84. This prophet was bald—according to one group of rude young guys, at least:
   a) Moses
   b) Elisha
   c) Joel
   d) Isaiah

85. At the Mount of Transfiguration, he offered to build three altars:

__ __ __ __ __

86. He killed 185,000 Assyrian warriors in one night:
    a) an angel of the Lord
    b) Elijah
    c) Hezekiah
    d) Samson

87. He lied and said he wanted to worship the baby Jesus: __ __ __ __ __

88. True or False: Thomas had his doubts in prison, so he sent messengers to Jesus.

89. He spotted a ram caught in the bushes:
   a) Ishmael
   b) Jacob
   c) an angel
   d) Abraham

90. He wrote the book of Colossians:

— — — —

91. She secretly lay down at the feet of a man she'd recently met:
   a) Ruth
   b) Esther
   c) Naomi
   d) Rahab

92. He was the humblest man on earth, according to a Bible book he wrote:

— — — — —

93. This man was so shy that he hid whenever he was chosen as king:
   a) Ahab
   b) Josiah
   c) Saul
   d) Hezekiah

94. True or False: Othniel's name was changed to Jerubbaal.

95. This woman was definitely at a wedding in Cana with Jesus:
   a) his mother
   b) Susanna
   c) Mary Magdalene
   d) Salome

96. True or False: In Genesis, the sons of Gabriel fell in love with the daughters of men.

97. This "son of the morning" tried to take God's place. . .and failed:

— — — — — — —

98. He was worthy to open the seven seals:
   a) the Lion of the tribe of Judah
   b) the angel who stood on sea and land
   c) one of the saints before the throne
   d) John

99. In Revelation, there were two of them, and they breathed fire:

— — — — — — — — — —

100. True or False: Saul (soon to be called Paul) escaped the Jews by tunneling under a wall.

WE HOPE
YOU'RE A GOOD
GUESSER

1. He had a rod (a walking stick) that popped out buds and blossoms:

   — — — — —

2. He offered some angelic assistance against the prince of Persia:
   a) Michael
   b) Gabriel
   c) Lucifer
   d) Raphael

3. His rebellion against Moses came to a ground-shaking end:

   — — — — —

4. She sold purple cloth:
   a) Anna
   b) Esther
   c) Lydia
   d) Ruth

5. True or False: Ezekiel inserted a bread recipe into his book of prophecy.

6. He shared his house with the ark of God for three months:
   a) Obadiah
   b) David
   c) Obededom
   d) Phinehas

7. True or False: Timothy's grandmother was named Eunice.

8. He was a crippled young man whom David helped:

   __ __ __ __ __ __ __ __

   __ __ __ __ __

9. This man made silver idols in Ephesus:

— — — — — — — — —

10. He parted the Jordan with a coat:
   a) Elijah
   b) Elisha
   c) Elihu
   d) Eleazar

11. True or False: Obadiah once hid a hundred prophets in a cave.

12. This man disagreed with Paul over whether or not to take Mark on a missionary trip:
   a) Luke
   b) Barabbas
   c) Barnabas
   d) Silas

13. He had really big handwriting:

___ ___ ___ ___

14. These people couldn't pronounce a password correctly:
   a) Hittites
   b) Philistines
   c) Ephraimites
   d) Levites

15. This future king was well known for his reckless chariot driving:

___ ___ ___ ___

16. These two mythical figures were displayed on Paul's ship to Rome:
   a) Jupiter and Mercury
   b) Baal and Asherah
   c) Chemosh and Molech
   d) Castor and Pollux

17. True or False: Bathsheba once talked David out of taking revenge.

18. This less well-known prophet prophesied two years before an earthquake:
    a) Obadiah
    b) Hosea
    c) Amos
    d) Zechariah

19. He multiplied a widow's cooking oil:

    — — — — — —

20. True or False: A woman named Michal got angry when she saw her husband dancing.

21. True or False: King Saul disobeyed orders by eating honey.

22. He was renamed Belteshazzar:

__ __ __ __ __ __

23. This ruler became friends with Pontius Pilate after Jesus' trial:
   a) Herod
   b) Nero
   c) Agrippa
   d) Joseph of Arimathea

24. His descendants were cursed by Noah because he saw Noah naked:

__ __ __

25. True or False: Lot's daughters didn't believe his warning about the coming destruction of Sodom.

26. This person was the first recipient of Luke's Gospel:
   a) Agrippa
   b) Theophilus
   c) Felix
   d) The elect lady

27. She changed her name to Mara out of sadness: __ __ __ __ __

28. True or False: Amasa died after being stabbed in the eye.

29. This unnamed person ran away naked during Jesus' arrest:
a) a young man
b) a blind man
c) a rich young ruler
d) a man with a withered hand

30. This New Testament prophet predicted a famine:

__ __ __ __ __ __

31. True or False: Philip had seven daughters who prophesied.

32. This apostle did something wrong in Antioch that caused Paul to oppose him: __ __ __ __ __

33. They fooled Joshua with old belongings and moldy bread:
   a) the Jebusites
   b) the people of Gibeon
   c) the people of Israel
   d) the Ammonites

34. True or False: Phinehas got his name because the glory was departed from Israel.

35. She married Moses:
   a) Shiphrah
   b) Zipporah
   c) Puah
   d) Hannah

36. He wrote a letter to "the elect lady and her children": __ __ __ __

37. True or False: Joab died because his hair got caught in a tree.

38. She came with King Agrippa to Paul's trial: __ __ __ __ __ __ __

39. This judge drew a sword with his left hand:
   a) Ehud
   b) Samson
   c) Shamgar
   d) Othniel

40. True or False: In the story the prophet Nathan told King David, a poor man steals a sheep.

41. Abishai, a military leader, wanted David's permission to kill this man:

—— —— —— ——

42. He had a huge bed of iron:
a) Goliath
b) Ahab
c) Og
d) Pharaoh

43. True or False: Nabal's heart died (and so did he) when his wife gave him some scary news.

44. He lost a chariot race to Elijah. . .who was on foot:
a) Elisha
b) Isaiah
c) King Ahab
d) Elijah's servant

45. He prophesied about old men dreaming dreams and young men seeing visions:
a) Amos
b) Obadiah
c) Joel
d) Haggai

46. She lived under a palm tree in the mountains:

— — — — — — —

47. True or False: A man named Shimei cursed at King David.

48. He walked in backwards with Japheth to cover Noah up so that he wouldn't see the old man naked.
a) Shem
b) Gershom
c) Ham
d) Methuselah

49. She gave birth to Moses:

__ __ __ __ __ __ __ __

50. True or False: David gave cedars to Solomon to help him build the temple.

51. This king was blinded and carried off as a prisoner into Babylon.
   a) Ahab
   b) Rehoboam
   c) Zedekiah
   d) Josiah

52. This new king ignored the old guys' advice in favor of the younger guys' ideas:

__ __ __ __ __ __ __ __

53. When the disciples picked out a replacement for Judas, this man lost out to Matthias:
   a) Paul
   b) James, Jesus' brother
   c) Joseph, also called Barsabbas Justus
   d) Apollos

54. He was Lot's dad:

   __ __ __ __ __

55. True or False: Jesus' twelve disciples buried John the Baptist's body.

56. God opened the eyes of this man's servant so that he could see a divine army:
   a) Elijah
   b) Elihu
   c) Elisha
   d) Eliazar

57. Sennacherib, king of this country, was killed by his sons:

— — — — — — —

58. True or False: Jeremiah prophesied that Babylon would rule over Israel for seventy years.

59. He was convinced that David had gone insane:
a) Goliath
b) Achan
c) Achish
d) Jonathan

60. She was Hosea's unfaithful wife:

— — — — —

61. True or False: Luke's Gospel describes Jesus bringing Lazarus back to life.

62. This man's tribe of Israel eventually included the apostle Paul:
    a) Benjamin
    b) Judah
    c) Reuben
    d) Naphtali

63. He was Job's fourth friend who chimed in near the end:

    __ __ __ __ __

64. He was originally known as Azariah:
    a) Ananias
    b) Abraham
    c) Aquila
    d) Abednego

65. True or False: Job's bones brought a man back to life when they touched his body.

66. This apostle seemingly had a miraculous shadow:

— — — — —

67. This prophet, following God's orders, hid his belt in a hole in the rock:
   a) Daniel
   b) Hosea
   c) Nahum
   d) Jeremiah

68. Golden statues of these angelic creatures covered the ark of God:

— — — — — — — —

69. True or False: Esau married two women his parents didn't approve of.

70. His words are written in Proverbs 31:
  a) Solomon
  b) Lemuel
  c) Asaph
  d) Malachi

71. He argued with the devil over Moses' body:

— — — — — — —

72. True or False: The people of Jericho were few, but they scared off 3,000 Israelite soldiers.

73. They were "bewitched" (a King James Version word meaning tricked) into not believing the truth:
  - a) Corinthians
  - b) Galatians
  - c) Ephesians
  - d) Thessalonians

74. His children died when the wind blew down their house: __ __ __

75. His story was used by Jesus to explain His own burial and resurrection:
  - a) Adam
  - b) Joel
  - c) Hezekiah
  - d) Jonah

76. He was in the Spirit on the Lord's Day when he received a revelation:

__ __ __ __

77. True or False: Nehemiah beat up some disobedient guys and pulled out their hair.

78. This queen refused to go to King Ahasuerus' party—and he was furious:
   a) Esther
   b) Vashti
   c) Jezebel
   d) Queen of Sheba

79. He had a vision about trying to cross a river that became too deep:

__ __ __ __ __ __ __

80. True or False: In Revelation, a many-headed woman rose up out of the sea.

81. Only 600 men from this tribe survived a war:
   a) Ephraim
   b) Manasseh
   c) Benjamin
   d) Zebulun

82. This king announced that he'd worship Baal. . .but he was setting a trap:

— — — —

83. This guy had a bunch of gods, but believed it was okay because he had hired a Levite priest:
   a) the good Samaritan
   b) Micah
   c) King Joash
   d) Mordecai

84. True or False: Mary Magdalene once had seven demons living inside her.

85. He spoke "woes"—words of criticism and warning—over the towns of Chorazin and Bethsaida:

__ __ __ __ __

86. These "inner circle" disciples went with Jesus to the Mount of Transfiguration:
   a) Thaddeus, Peter, and Jude
   b) Andrew, Jude, and John
   c) Peter, James, and John
   d) John, Peter, and Judas

87. He insulted the high priest, not knowing who he was, then had to apologize: __ __ __ __

88. His daughters Jemimah, Keziah, and Keren-happuch were the most beautiful women in the land:

__ __ __

89. These men jumped out of the bushes to catch young women to marry:
   a) the children of Judah
   b) the children of Abraham
   c) the children of Benjamin
   d) the children of Naphtali

90. His mother-in-law was sick, so Jesus healed her: __ __ __ __ __

91. His friends told him not to enter a theater because it was too dangerous:

__ __ __ __

92. This lesser-known prophet wrote a book about how Nineveh would be destroyed:
   a) Zephaniah
   b) Obadiah
   c) Haggai
   d) Nahum

93. True or False: A man named Abimelech killed 69 of his 70 brothers.

94. This king of Judah gave the Babylonians a guided tour of his house:

— — — — — — — —

95. She hid idols under her camel saddle:
   a) Delilah
   b) Rachel
   c) Jezebel
   d) Ruth

96. True or False: David had two sons named Gershom and Eliezer.

97. He carved marks in sticks and placed them in front of a livestock watering hole: __ __ __ __ __

98. She hung a red rope out her window:
a) Esther
b) Hannah
c) Rahab
d) Mary Magdalene

99. True or False: The Israelites saw red water and thought a bloody battle had happened.

100. He replaced Belshazzar as king in Babylon:
a) Rehoboam
b) Felix
c) Hezekiah
d) Darius the Mede

ANSWER KEY

TOO EASY! ANSWER KEY

1. **c)** And in the fourth watch of the night **Jesus** went unto them, walking on the sea. (Matthew 14:25 KJV)

2. The man called his wife's name **Eve**, because she was the mother of all living. (Genesis 3:20 NLV)

3. **False:** So the king had **Daniel** brought in and thrown into the place where lions were kept. (Daniel 6:16 NLV)

4. Now Israel loved **Joseph** more than all his children, because he was the son of his old age, and he made him a coat of many colors. (Genesis 37:3 SKJV)

5. **b)** But **Pharaoh** said, "Who is the Lord, that I should obey Him and let Israel go? I do not know the Lord. And I will not let Israel go." (Exodus 5:2 NLV)

6. **True:** And God said to **Noah**. . ."Make an ark of gopher wood." (Genesis 6:13–14 SKJV)

7. **a)** Then **Esther** spoke again to the king. She fell at his feet and cried and begged him to stop the sinful plan of Haman the Agagite, the plan he had made against the Jews. (Esther 8:3 NLV)

8. And the LORD said unto Satan, Hast thou considered my servant **Job**, that there is none like him in the earth, a perfect and an upright man, one that feareth God, and escheweth evil? (Job 1:8 KJV)

9. **b)** And **Gideon** said to God, "If You will save Israel by my hand, as You have said—behold, I will put a fleece of wool on the threshing floor, and if the dew is on the fleece only, and it is dry on all the earth beside it, then I shall know that You will save Israel by my hand, as You have said." (Judges 6:36–37 SKJV)

10. **False:** And they said, Is not this Jesus, the son of **Joseph**, whose father and mother we know? (John 6:42 KJV)

11. Then **David** ran and stood over the Philistine. He took his sword out of its holder and killed him, and cut off his head with it. (1 Samuel 17:51 NLV)

12. **False:** Neither shall thy name any more be called Abram, but thy name shall be **Abraham**; for a father of many nations have I made thee. (Genesis 17:5 KJV)

13. **b)** And when they were in the field, **Cain** stood up against his brother Abel and killed

him. (Genesis 4:8 NLV)

14. **True:** When **Pilate** saw that he could prevail nothing, but that rather a tumult was made, he took water, and washed his hands before the multitude, saying, I am innocent of the blood of this just person. (Matthew 27:24 KJV)

15. **b)** And one of **the criminals who was hanged** railed on Him, saying, "If You are Christ, save Yourself and us." But the other. . . said to Jesus, "Lord, remember me when You come into Your kingdom." (Luke 23:39–40, 42 SKJV)

16. The Lord **God** planted a garden to the east in Eden. (Genesis 2:8 NLV)

17. **c)** So king **Solomon** exceeded all the kings of the earth for riches and for wisdom. (1 Kings 10:23 KJV)

18. **False:** So Delilah said to **Samson**, "I beg you. Tell me the secret of your powerful strength.". . . She asked him day after day until his soul was troubled to death. So he told her all that was in his mind. (Judges 16:6, 16–17 NLV)

19. The hand of the LORD was on me and carried me out in the Spirit of the LORD, and set me

down in the midst of the valley that was full of bones. (**Ezekiel** 37:1 SKJV)

20. **a)** Now the word of the LORD came to **Jonah**, the son of Amittai, saying, "Arise, go to Nineveh, that great city, and cry against it, for their wickedness has come up before Me." (Jonah 1:1–2 SKJV)

21. And it came to pass, as they still went on, and talked, that, behold, there appeared a chariot of fire, and horses of fire, and parted them both asunder; and **Elijah** went up by a whirlwind into heaven. (2 Kings 2:11 KJV)

22. **True:** "Woe to that man by whom the Son of Man is betrayed! It would have been good for that man if he had not been born." Then **Judas**, who betrayed Him, answered and said, "Master, is it I?" (Matthew 26:24–25 SKJV)

23. **c)** There was a rich man named **Zaccheus**. He was a leader of those who gathered taxes. Zaccheus wanted to see Jesus but he could not because so many people were there and he was a short man. (Luke 19:2–3 NLV)

24. The LORD said to **Joshua**, "See, I have given into your hand Jericho, and its king, and the mighty men of valor. And you shall surround the city, all you men of war, and go around the city once. You shall do this for six days." (Joshua 6:2–3 SKJV)

25. **True:** But **Thomas**, one of the twelve, called Didymus, was not with them when Jesus came. The other disciples therefore said unto him, We have seen the LORD. But he said unto them, Except I shall see in his hands the print of the nails, and put my finger into the print of the nails, and thrust my hand into his side, I will not believe. (John 20:24–25 KJV)

26. **c)** Through Adam's sin, death and hell came to all men. But another Man, **Christ**, by His right act makes men free and gives them life. (Romans 5:18 NLV)

27. **c)** She saw the basket in the tall grass and sent the woman who served her to get it. She opened it and saw the child. . . . She gave him the name **Moses**, saying, "Because I took him out of the water." (Exodus 2:5–6, 10 NLV)

28. **False:** From the roof he saw a woman washing herself. The woman was very beautiful. So David sent someone to ask about the woman. And one said, "Is this not

Eliam's daughter **Bathsheba**?" (2 Samuel 11:2–3 NLV)

29. **Adam** and his wife hid themselves from the presence of the LORD God among the trees of the garden. (Genesis 3:8 SKJV)

30. **a)** And they cried out all at once, saying, Away with [Jesus], and release unto us **Barabbas**. (Luke 23:18 KJV)

31. And the Lord opened the mouth of the **donkey**, and she said to Balaam, "What have I done to you? Why have you hit me these three times?" (Numbers 22:28 NLV)

32. **True:** And the bow shall be in the cloud; and I will look upon it, that I may remember the everlasting covenant between God and every living creature of all flesh that is upon the earth. And God said unto **Noah**, This is the token of the covenant. (Genesis 9:16–17 KJV)

33. **b)** And Elijah said to **the prophets of Baal**, "Choose one bull for yourselves and prepare it first, for you are many, and call on the name of your gods, but put no fire under it." (1 Kings 18:25 SKJV)

34. By faith the harlot **Rahab** perished not

with them that believed not, when she had received the spies with peace. (Hebrews 11:31 KJV)

35. **False:** This is **John** writing to the seven churches in the country of Asia. (Revelation 1:4 NLV)

36. **d)** So **Boaz** took Ruth, and she was his wife. (Ruth 4:13 SKJV)

37. **False:** And as he journeyed, he came near **Damascus:** and suddenly there shined round about him a light from heaven: And he fell to the earth, and heard a voice saying unto him, Saul, Saul, why persecutest thou me? (Acts 9:3–4 KJV)

38. The birth of Jesus Christ was like this: **Mary** His mother had been promised in marriage to Joseph. (Matthew 1:18 NLV)

39. **d)** God said, "Take now your son, your only son, **Isaac,** whom you love. . . . Give him as a burnt gift on the altar in worship, on one of the mountains I will show you." (Genesis 22:2 NLV)

40. And there were in the same country **shepherds** abiding in the field, keeping watch over their flock by night. And, lo, the

angel of the Lord came upon them, and the glory of the Lord shone round about them: and they were sore afraid. (Luke 2:8–9 KJV)

41. **c)** The **demons** asked Him saying, "Send us to the pigs that we may go into them." Then Jesus let them do what they wanted to do. So they went into the pigs. The pigs ran fast down the side of the mountain and into the sea and died. There were about 2,000. (Mark 5:12–13 NLV)

42. Then cometh **Jesus** from Galilee to Jordan unto John, to be baptized of him. (Matthew 3:13 KJV)

43. **False:** And Jonah began to enter into the city a day's journey, and he cried, and said, Yet forty days, and Nineveh shall be overthrown. So **the people of Nineveh** believed God, and proclaimed a fast, and put on sackcloth, from the greatest of them even to the least of them. (Jonah 3:4–5 KJV)

44. **b)** And **Saul** cast the javelin; for he said, I will smite David even to the wall with it. And David avoided out of his presence twice. (1 Samuel 18:11 KJV)

45. About midnight Paul and Silas were praying and singing songs of thanks to God. The

other men in **prison** were listening to them. (Acts 16:25 NLV)

46. **b)** Then entered **Satan** into Judas surnamed Iscariot, being of the number of the twelve. And he went his way, and communed with the chief priests and captains, how he might betray him unto them. (Luke 22:3–4 KJV)

47. **d)** The **children of Israel** walked on dry land in the midst of the sea, and the waters were a wall to them on their right hand and on their left. (Exodus 14:29 SKJV)

48. **True:** But a certain **Samaritan**, as he journeyed, came where he was: and when he saw him, he had compassion on him, and went to him, and bound up his wounds, pouring in oil and wine, and set him on his own beast, and brought him to an inn, and took care of him. (Luke 10:33–34 KJV)

49. Now when Jesus was born in Bethlehem of Judaea in the days of Herod the king, behold, there came **wise men** from the east to Jerusalem, saying, Where is he that is born King of the Jews? for we have seen his star in the east, and are come to worship him. (Matthew 2:1–2 KJV)

50. **c)** Now when Job's three **friends** heard of all this trouble that had come upon him, they came each from his own place. (Job 2:11 NLV)

51. **False:** And the Egyptians could not drink of the water of the river. And there was blood throughout all the land of Egypt. And **the magicians of Egypt** did so with their enchantments. (Exodus 7:21–22 SKJV)

52. Jesus said, "I tell you, **Peter**, a rooster will not crow today before you will say three times that you do not know Me." (Luke 22:34 NLV)

53. **True:** These are the wise sayings of **Solomon**, son of David, king of Israel. (Proverbs 1:1 NLV)

54. The Lord said to **Moses**. . . "Your brother Aaron will be the one who speaks for you." (Exodus 7:1 NLV)

55. c) Then **the Lord** poured fire from the heavens upon Sodom and Gomorrah. He destroyed those cities. (Genesis 19:24–25 NLV)

56. **True: Samson** said, "Let me die with the Philistines." And he pushed with all his might, and the house fell on the lords and on all the people who were in it. (Judges 16:30 SKJV)

57. But the angel said unto him, Fear not, Zacharias: for thy prayer is heard; and thy

wife **Elisabeth** shall bear thee a son, and
thou shalt call his name John. (Luke 1:13 KJV)

58. **a)** And **Jacob** loved Rachel; and said,
I will serve thee seven years for Rachel
thy younger daughter. (Genesis 29:18 KJV)

59. When the queen of **Sheba** heard about
the wisdom Solomon had from the Lord,
she came to test him with hard questions.
(1 Kings 10:1 NLV)

60. **c)** "But woe to you, scribes and **Pharisees**,
hypocrites! For you shut up the kingdom of
heaven against men." (Matthew 23:13 SKJV)

61. **True:** Therefore Pilate then took **Jesus**
and scourged Him. And the soldiers wove
a crown of thorns and put it on His head.
(John 19:1–2 SKJV)

62. **c)** Then **Jonah** prayed unto the LORD his
God out of the fish's belly. (Jonah 2:1 KJV)

63. Then **Nebuchadnezzar** the king was
astonished and rose up quickly and spoke
and said to his counselors, "Did we not cast
three men bound into the midst of the
fire? . . . Look, I see four men loose,
walking in the midst of the fire."
(Daniel 3:24–25 SKJV)

64. **False:** And immediately something like scales fell from his eyes, and he received sight immediately and arose and was baptized. And when he had received food, he was strengthened. Then for some days **Saul** was with the disciples who were at Damascus. (Acts 9:18–19 SKJV)

65. **b)** And Adam knew **Eve** his wife; and she conceived, and bare Cain, and said, I have gotten a man from the LORD. And she again bare his brother Abel. (Genesis 4:1–2 KJV)

66. And the battle went sore against Saul, and the archers hit him; and he was sore wounded of the archers. Then said **Saul** unto his armourbearer, Draw thy sword, and thrust me through therewith. (1 Samuel 31:3–4 KJV)

67. **False:** After the death of the Lord's servant Moses, the Lord said to Moses' helper, **Joshua**. . . "My servant Moses is dead. So you and all these people get up and cross the Jordan River to the land I am giving to the people of Israel." (Joshua 1:1–2 NLV)

68. **c)** "But **the man who gathered taxes** stood a long way off. He would not even lift his eyes to heaven. But he hit himself on his

chest and said, 'God, have pity on me! I am a sinner!' I tell you, this man went back to his house forgiven, and not the other man." (Luke 18:13–14 NLV)

69. **a)** The word of the LORD came expressly unto **Ezekiel** the priest, the son of Buzi, in the land of the Chaldeans by the river Chebar; and the hand of the LORD was there upon him. (Ezekiel 1:3 KJV)

70. **b)** [God] raised up unto them David to be their king; to whom also he gave their testimony, and said, I have found **David**. . .a man after mine own heart, which shall fulfil all my will. (Acts 13:22 KJV)

71. And it came to pass at the time of the offering of the evening sacrifice, that **Elijah** the prophet came near, and said. . . Hear me, O LORD, hear me, that this people may know that thou art the LORD God, and that thou hast turned their heart back again. Then the fire of the LORD fell, and consumed the burnt sacrifice. (1 Kings 18:36–38 KJV)

72. **False:** And the LORD God caused a deep sleep to fall upon **Adam**, and he slept: and he took one of his ribs, and closed up the flesh instead thereof; And the rib, which the

LORD God had taken from man, made he a woman. (Genesis 2:21–22 KJV)

73. **c)** Then answered they and said before the king, That **Daniel**, which is of the children of the captivity of Judah, regardeth not thee, O king, nor the decree that thou hast signed, but maketh his petition three times a day. (Daniel 6:13 KJV)

74. **Moses** looked and saw that the bush was burning with fire, but it was not being burned up. (Exodus 3:2 NLV)

75. **b) Christ** was buried. He was raised from the dead three days later as the Holy Writings said He would. (1 Corinthians 15:4 NLV)

76. **True: Paul**. . .unto the church of God which is at Corinth. . . . Lest I should be exalted above measure through the abundance of the revelations, there was given to me a thorn in the flesh. (2 Corinthians 1:1; 12:7 KJV)

77. And the LORD had respect unto **Abel** and to his offering: but unto Cain and to his offering he had not respect. (Genesis 4:4–5 KJV)

78. **b)** And **Enoch** walked with God, and he was not, for God took him. (Genesis 5:24 SKJV)

79. **False:** In all this **Job** did not sin with his lips. (Job 2:10 SKJV)

80. Then thus came every maiden unto the king. . . . And the king loved **Esther** above all the women. . .so that he set the royal crown upon her head, and made her queen. (Esther 2:13, 17 KJV)

81. **a)** Jesus said, "You told the truth when you said, 'I have no husband.' You have had five husbands." (John 4:17–18 NLV)

82. Then **Jacob** was left alone. And a man fought with him until morning. . . . So Jacob gave the place the name of Peniel. For he said, "I have seen God face to face." (Genesis 32:24, 30 NLV)

83. **d)** Then **Isaac** brought Rebekah into his mother Sarah's tent, and she became his wife. (Genesis 24:67 NLV)

84. **False:** Then came there **two women**. . .unto the king, and stood before him. And the one woman said, O my lord, I and this woman dwell in one house; and I was delivered of a child with her in the house. (1 Kings 3:16–17 KJV)

85. Then **Jesus** went into the house of God and

made all those leave who were buying and selling there. He turned over the tables of the men who changed money. He turned over the seats of those who sold doves. (Matthew 21:12 NLV)

86. **True:** And when the day of Pentecost had fully come, they were all with one accord in one place. . . . And they were all filled with the **Holy Spirit** and began to speak with other tongues, as the Spirit gave them speech. (Acts 2:1, 4 SKJV)

87. **a) The LORD** caused the sea to go back by a strong east wind all that night, and made the sea dry land, and the waters were divided. (Exodus 14:21 KJV)

88. Jesus said to them, "I saw **Satan** fall from heaven like lightning." (Luke 10:18 NLV)

89. Then **Pharaoh** told all his people, "Throw every son who is born to the Hebrews into the Nile. But keep every daughter alive." (Exodus 1:22 NLV)

90. **False:** And out of the ground the LORD God formed every beast of the field, and every fowl of the air; and brought them unto Adam to see what he would call them: and whatsoever **Adam** called every

living creature, that was the name thereof.
(Genesis 2:19 KJV)

91. **b) Herod**. . .was very angry. He sent men
to kill all the young boys two years old and
under in Bethlehem and in all the country
near by. (Matthew 2:16 NLV)

92. **False:** Jesus was led by the Holy Spirit to a
desert. There He was tempted by **the devil**.
(Matthew 4:1 NLV)

93. **b)** "The Helper (**Holy Spirit**) will tell about
Me when He comes. I will send Him to you
from the Father. He is the Spirit of Truth
and comes from the Father."
(John 15:26 NLV)

94. **a)** And it came to pass in those days, that
there went out a decree from **Caesar
Augustus** that all the world should be taxed.
(Luke 2:1 KJV)

95. And **Moses** wrote this law and delivered
it to the priests, the sons of Levi, who bore
the ark of the covenant of the LORD,
and to all the elders of Israel.
(Deuteronomy 31:9 SKJV)

96. **True:** The **fool** hath said in his heart, There
is no God. They are corrupt, they have done

abominable works, there is none that doeth good. (Psalm 14:1 KJV)

97. **c)** And God saw their works, that they turned from their evil way; and God repented of the evil, that he had said that he would do unto them; and he did it not. But it displeased **Jonah** exceedingly, and he was very angry. (Jonah 3:10–4:1 KJV)

98. The devil came tempting Him and said, "If You are the Son of God, tell these stones to be made into bread." But **Jesus** said, "It is written, 'Man is not to live on bread only. Man is to live by every word that God speaks.'" (Matthew 4:3–4 NLV)

99. **b)** Then **Moses** put out his hand over the sea. And the Lord moved the sea all night by a strong east wind. So the waters were divided. (Exodus 14:21 NLV)

100. **True:** For **God** so loved the world that He gave His only Son. Whoever puts his trust in God's Son will not be lost but will have life that lasts forever. (John 3:16 NLV)

A LITTLE TOUGHER
ANSWER KEY

1. But **Lot**'s wife behind him turned and looked toward the cities. And she was changed into salt. (Genesis 19:26 NLV)

2. **d) Paul**, a servant of Jesus Christ, called to be an apostle, separated unto the gospel of God. (Romans 1:1 KJV)

3. **True:** Then Samuel took a bottle of oil and poured it on **Saul**'s head. He kissed him and said, "Has not the Lord chosen you to be a ruler over His land?" (1 Samuel 10:1 NLV)

4. And as Jesus passed forth from there, He saw a man named **Matthew** sitting at the place where tax was collected. And He said to him, "Follow Me." And he arose and followed Him. (Matthew 9:9 SKJV)

5. **b)** Jesus said, "Come!" **Peter** got out of the boat and walked on the water to Jesus. (Matthew 14:29 NLV)

6. And Jacob did so and fulfilled her week, and he gave him **Rachel** his daughter as a wife also. . . . And he also loved Rachel more than Leah. (Genesis 29:28, 30 SKJV)

7. **False:** And it came to pass in those days, when Moses was grown, that he went out to his brothers and saw their burdens. And he spied an **Egyptian** striking a Hebrew, one of his brothers. (Exodus 2:11 SKJV)

8. **False:** And James the son of Zebedee, and John the brother of James; and he surnamed them Boanerges, which is, The **sons of thunder**. (Mark 3:17 KJV)

9. When He had said this, He called with a loud voice, "**Lazarus**, come out!" The man who had been dead came out. His hands and feet were tied in grave clothes. A white cloth was tied around his face. (John 11:43–44 NLV)

10. **d)** In the beginning was the Word, and the Word was with God, and the Word was God. (**John** 1:1 KJV); In the beginning God created the heaven and the earth. (Genesis 1:1 KJV)

11. **a)** Then **his wife** said to him, "Do you still hold on to your faith? Curse God and die!" (Job 2:9 NLV)

12. **True:** And **Joshua** the son of Nun was full of the spirit of wisdom, for Moses had laid his hands on him. (Deuteronomy 34:9 SKJV)

13. And when they came to Nachon's

threshingfloor, **Uzzah** put forth his hand to the ark of God, and took hold of it; for the oxen shook it. And the anger of the LORD was kindled against Uzzah; and God smote him there for his error; and there he died by the ark of God. (2 Samuel 6:6–7 KJV)

14. **True: Christ** made everything in the heavens and on the earth. (Colossians 1:16 NLV)

15. **b)** Then Zeresh his wife and all his friends said to him, "Let a gallows be made fifty cubits high, and tomorrow say to the king that **Mordecai** be hanged on it." (Esther 5:14 SKJV)

16. And Joseph was brought down to Egypt; and **Potiphar**, an officer of Pharaoh, captain of the guard, an Egyptian, bought him of the hands of the Ishmeelites, which had brought him down thither. (Genesis 39:1 KJV)

17. **d)** Abram was eighty-six years old when **Hagar** gave birth to his son Ishmael. (Genesis 16:16 NLV)

18. **False:** So all the people took the gold objects from their ears and brought them to Aaron. He took the gold from their hands, worked on it with a sharp tool, and by melting it, made it into a calf. Then they said, "This is

your god, O **Israel**, who brought you out of the land of Egypt." (Exodus 32:3–4 NLV)

19. The priests the Levites, and all the tribe of **Levi**, shall have no part nor inheritance with Israel: they shall eat the offerings of the LORD made by fire, and his inheritance. (Deuteronomy 18:1 KJV)

20. b) Then **Nebuchadnezzar** was filled with anger. . . . He had the fire made seven times hotter than it was. (Daniel 3:19 NLV)

21. Therefore the Lord himself shall give you a sign; Behold, a virgin shall conceive, and bear a son, and shall call his name Immanuel. (**Isaiah** 7:14 KJV)

22. **False:** Then Agrippa said unto **Paul,** Almost thou persuadest me to be a Christian. (Acts 26:28 KJV)

23. b) Then **Jezebel** sent news to Elijah, saying, "So may the gods do to me and even more, if I do not make your life as the life of one of them by this time tomorrow." Elijah was afraid. He got up and ran for his life. (1 Kings 19:2–3 NLV)

24. Mary stood outside the grave crying. As she cried, she got down and looked inside the

grave. She saw two **angels** dressed in white clothes. They were sitting where the body of Jesus had lain. (John 20:11–12 NLV)

25. **a)** Then the Lord said to Abraham, "Why did **Sarah** laugh and say, 'How can I give birth to a child when I am so old?'" (Genesis 18:13 NLV)

26. **False:** And he gave unto **Moses**, when he had made an end of communing with him upon mount Sinai, two tables of testimony, tables of stone, written with the finger of God. (Exodus 31:18 KJV)

27. But Naomi said, "Return to your people, my daughters." . . . But **Ruth** held on to her. (Ruth 1:11, 14 NLV)

28. **c)** In Gibeon **the LORD** appeared to Solomon in a dream by night. (1 Kings 3:5 SKJV)

29. **False:** The soul of **Jonathan** was knit with the soul of David, and Jonathan loved him as his own soul. (1 Samuel 18:1 KJV)

30. "**Saul** has seen a man called Ananias in a dream. He is to come and put his hands on Saul so he might see again." (Acts 9:12 NLV)

31. **False:** His servants said to him, "See, there

is a woman at Endor who can speak with spirits." So **Saul** dressed up to look like somebody else and went with two other men to the woman during the night. (1 Samuel 28:7–8 NLV)

32. **True: Abraham** said to the oldest servant in his house. . . "Go to my country and to those of my family. Take a wife for my son Isaac from there." (Genesis 24:2, 4 NLV)

33. John had said unto **Herod**, It is not lawful for thee to have thy brother's wife. (Mark 6:18 KJV)

34. **d)** So they took Jeremiah and put him into the well of Malchijah the king's son, in the open space of the prison, letting him down with ropes. There was no water in the well, but only mud. And **Jeremiah** went down into the mud. (Jeremiah 38:6 NLV)

35. **b)** And when they were come up out of the water, the Spirit of the Lord caught away **Philip**. (Acts 8:39 KJV)

36. **False:** And he arose and came to his father. But when he was still a great way off, **his father** saw him and had compassion, and ran and fell on his neck and kissed him. (Luke 15:20 SKJV)

37. After two years had passed, **Pharaoh** had a dream. He dreamed that he was standing by the Nile River. And he saw seven cows coming out of the Nile. (Genesis 41:1–2 NLV)

38. **c)** David put on his sword over his heavy battle-clothes and tried to walk, for he was not used to them. Then **David** said to Saul, "I cannot go with these, for I am not used to them." And David took them off. He took his stick in his hand, and chose five smooth stones from the river. (1 Samuel 17:39–40 NLV)

39. **False: Nathan** said to David, "You are the man! . . . 'Why have you hated the Word of the Lord by doing what is bad in His eyes?'" (2 Samuel 12:7, 9 NLV)

40. **Jacob** went out from Beersheba, and went toward Haran. . . . And he dreamed, and behold a ladder set up on the earth, and the top of it reached to heaven. (Genesis 28:10, 12 KJV)

41. **c)** They got up and took **Jesus** out of town to the top of a high hill. They wanted to throw Him over the side. But Jesus got away from among them and went on His way. (Luke 4:29–30 NLV)

42. **False:** Then God said to Abraham, "As for **Sarai** your wife, do not call her name Sarai. But Sarah will be her name." (Genesis 17:15 NLV)

43. Now the turn came for **Esther**, the daughter of Abihail, the brother of the father of Mordecai who had taken her as his daughter, to go in to the king. (Esther 2:15 NLV)

44. **c) Luke**, the dear doctor. (Colossians 4:14 NLV)

45. **True:** And when the day of Pentecost was fully come, they were all with one accord in one place. . . . **Peter**, standing up with the eleven, lifted up his voice, and said unto them, Ye men of Judaea, and all ye that dwell at Jerusalem, be this known unto you, and hearken to my words. (Acts 2:1, 14 KJV)

46. Then **Daniel** answered the king, saying, "Keep your gifts for yourself, or give them to someone else. But I will read the writing to the king and tell him what it means." (Daniel 5:17 NLV)

47. **b)** And Joshua the son of Nun and **Caleb** the son of Jephunneh tore their clothes. They were among those who had spied out the land. They said to all the people of Israel,

"The land we passed through to spy out is a very good land. If the Lord is pleased with us, then He will bring us into this land and give it to us." (Numbers 14:6–8 NLV)

48. **False: Joseph of Arimathaea**, an honourable counsellor, which also waited for the kingdom of God, came, and went in boldly unto Pilate, and craved the body of Jesus. (Mark 15:43 KJV)

49. **Abraham** said about his wife Sarah, "She is my sister.". . . Abraham said, "I did it because I thought there was no fear of God in this place. I thought they would kill me because of my wife." (Genesis 20:2, 11 NLV)

50. **False: Paul**, an apostle of Jesus Christ by the commandment of God our Saviour, and Lord Jesus Christ, which is our hope. (1 Timothy 1:1 KJV)

51. It came to pass, when they had crossed over, that Elijah said to Elisha, "Ask me what I should do for you before I am taken away from you." And **Elisha** said, "I ask, let a double portion of your spirit be upon me." (2 Kings 2:9 SKJV)

52. **b)** When the morning came, Jacob saw that it was **Leah**. He said. . . "What have

you done to me? Did I not work for you for Rachel? Why have you fooled me?" (Genesis 29:25 NLV)

53. **False:** Then the Lord said to **Moses,** "Go up to this mountain of Abarim, and see the land I have given to the people of Israel. When you have seen it, you will be buried with your people as Aaron your brother was." (Numbers 27:12–13 NLV)

54. **Josiah** was eight years old when he began to reign, and he reigned thirty-one years in Jerusalem. (2 Kings 22:1 SKJV)

55. **c)** So **Methuselah** lived 969 years, and he died. (Genesis 5:27 NLV)

56. "You will always travel from place to place on the earth." . . . **Cain** went away from the face of the Lord, and stayed in the land of Nod, east of Eden. (Genesis 4:12, 16 NLV)

57. **True:** But when **Herod** heard thereof, he said, It is John, whom I beheaded: he is risen from the dead. (Mark 6:16 KJV)

58. **b)** And there was one **Anna,** a prophetess. . . . And she was a widow of about fourscore and four years, which departed not from the temple, but served God with fastings and prayers night and day. (Luke 2:36–37 KJV)

59. But **Jonah** rose up to flee to Tarshish from the presence of the LORD and went down to Joppa. And he found a ship going to Tarshish, so he paid the fare and went down into it, to go with them to Tarshish from the presence of the LORD. (Jonah 1:3 SKJV)

60. **True:** The Song of Songs, the most beautiful of them all, which is **Solomon**'s. (Song of Solomon 1:1 NLV)

61. So they took **Joseph**'s coat, killed a male goat, and put the blood on the coat. They sent the coat of many colors to their father. And they said, "We found this. Is it your son's coat or not?" (Genesis 37:31–32 NLV)

62. **c) John** to the seven churches which are in Asia. . . . And I took the little book out of the angel's hand, and ate it up. (Revelation 1:4; 10:10 KJV)

63. **Gideon** took ten of his servants and did what the Lord had told him to do. But he was too afraid of those of his father's house and the men of the city to do it during the day. So he did it during the night. When the men of the city got up early in the morning, they saw that the altar of Baal was torn down. (Judges 6:27–28 NLV)

64. **a) Melchizedek** was without a father or mother or any family. He had no beginning of life or end of life. He is a religious leader forever like the Son of God. (Hebrews 7:3 NLV)

65. **False:** Now David was the son of **Jesse**, an Ephrathite of Bethlehem in Judah. (1 Samuel 17:12 NLV)

66. **Goliath** stood and called out to the army of Israel, saying. . . "I stand against the army of Israel this day. Give me a man, that we may fight together." (1 Samuel 17:8, 10 NLV)

67. **b)** There was a man of the Pharisees, named **Nicodemus**, a ruler of the Jews: The same came to Jesus by night, and said unto him, Rabbi, we know that thou art a teacher come from God: for no man can do these miracles that thou doest, except God be with him. (John 3:1–2 KJV)

68. But there was none like **Ahab** who sold himself to work wickedness in the sight of the LORD, whom his wife Jezebel stirred up. (1 Kings 21:25 SKJV)

69. **False: Deborah**, a prophetess, the wife of Lapidoth, judged Israel at that time. (Judges 4:4 SKJV)

70. **b)** Who can find **a virtuous woman**? For her price is far above rubies. (Proverbs 31:10 SKJV)

71. They were trying to set a trap to find something against Him. **Jesus** got down and began to write in the dust with His finger. (John 8:6 NLV)

72. **True:** And ere the lamp of God went out in the temple of the LORD, where the ark of God was, and **Samuel** was laid down to sleep; that the LORD called Samuel: and he answered, Here am I. And he ran unto Eli, and said, Here am I; for thou calledst me. (1 Samuel 3:3–5 KJV)

73. The Lord spoke to **Moses** face to face, as a man speaks to his friend. (Exodus 33:11 NLV)

74. **d)** And when **Paul** had gathered a bundle of sticks, and laid them on the fire, there came a viper out of the heat, and fastened on his hand. (Acts 28:3 KJV)

75. I planted, Apollos watered, but **God** gave the increase. (1 Corinthians 3:6 SKJV)

76. **b)** But we built the wall, and the whole wall was joined together to half its height, for the people had a mind to work. (**Nehemiah** 4:6 NLV)

77. **False:** "Return and tell **Hezekiah** the leader of My people, 'This is what the LORD, the God of David your father says: "I have heard your prayer. . . . And I will add fifteen years to your days."'" (2 Kings 20:5–6 SKJV)

78. And the man said, "Your name will no longer be **Jacob**, but Israel." (Genesis 32:28 NLV)

79. b) **Zacharias** said to the angel, "How can I know this for sure? I am old and my wife is old also." The angel said to him. . . "You will not be able to talk until the day this happens. It is because you did not believe my words." (Luke 1:18–20 NLV)

80. And as he entered into a certain village, there met him ten men that were **lepers**, which stood afar off: And they lifted up their voices, and said, Jesus, Master, have mercy on us. (Luke 17:12–13 KJV)

81. c) Then the LORD answered **Job** out of the whirlwind. (Job 38:1 SKJV)

82. **False:** Then all **the elders of Israel** gathered themselves together, and came to Samuel unto Ramah, and said unto him, Behold, thou art old, and thy sons walk not in thy ways: now make us a king to judge us like all the nations. (1 Samuel 8:4–5 KJV)

83. And the tablets were the work of God, and the writing was the writing of God, engraved on the tablets. . . . And **Moses**' anger grew hot, and he cast the tablets out of his hands and broke them beneath the mountain. (Exodus 32:16, 19 SKJV)

84. c) [An angel said,] "The boy will be a Nazirite to God from the time he is born to the time he dies." . . . Then the woman gave birth to a son and named him **Samson**. (Judges 13:7, 24 NLV)

85. **False:** And Paul dwelled **two whole years** in his own hired house, and received all who came to him. (Acts 28:30 SKJV)

86. c) And Nathan said unto David, The LORD also hath put away thy sin; thou shalt not die. Howbeit, because by this deed thou hast given great occasion to the enemies of the LORD to blaspheme, **the child also that is born unto thee** shall surely die. (2 Samuel 12:13–14 KJV)

87. Then assembled together the chief priests, and the scribes, and the elders of the people, unto the palace of the **high priest**, who was called Caiaphas, and consulted that they might take Jesus by subtilty, and kill him. (Matthew 26:3–4 KJV)

88. **c)** Every man according as he purposeth in his heart, so let him give; not grudgingly, or of necessity: for God loveth a cheerful **giver**. (2 Corinthians 9:7 KJV)

89. **False:** And it came to pass, when Moses came down from Mount Sinai with the two tablets of testimony in Moses' hand when he came down from the mountain, that **Moses** did not know that the skin of his face shone while he talked with Him. (Exodus 34:29 SKJV)

90. Then God spoke to them in a dream. He told them not to go back to Herod. So they went to their own country by another road. . . . Herod learned that the **wise men** had fooled him. (Matthew 2:12, 16 NLV)

91. **a)** So the Lord said to him, "Whoever kills Cain will be punished by Me seven times worse." And the Lord put a mark on **Cain** so that any one who found him would not kill him. (Genesis 4:15 NLV)

92. False: Nebuchadnezzar spake and said unto them, Is it true, O **Shadrach, Meshach, and Abednego**, do not ye serve my gods, nor worship the golden image which I have set up? (Daniel 3:14 KJV)

93. The book of the generation of Jesus Christ, the son of David, the son of Abraham. Abraham begat Isaac; and Isaac begat Jacob. . . (**Matthew** 1:1–2 KJV)

94. c) Then the devil went away from Jesus. **Angels** came and cared for Him. (Matthew 4:11 NLV)

95. True: Then David comforted his wife **Bathsheba**. . .and she gave birth to a son. He gave him the name Solomon. The Lord loved him. (2 Samuel 12:24 NLV)

96. Three days later there was a wedding in the town of Cana in the country of Galilee. . . . When the wine was all gone, the mother of Jesus said to Him, "They have no more wine." . . . **Jesus** said to the helpers, "Fill the jars with water." They filled them to the top. Then He said, "Take some out and give it to the head man who is caring for the people." They took some to him. The head man tasted the water that had become wine. (John 2:1, 3, 7–9 NLV)

97. **c)** And when the dew that lay had gone up, behold, on the face of the wilderness there lay a small round thing, as small as the white frost on the ground. And when **the children of Israel** saw it, they said one to another, "It is manna," for they did not know what it was. (Exodus 16:14–15 SKJV)

98. **False:** Now **King Solomon** loved many women from other nations. . . . He had 700 wives. (1 Kings 11:1, 3 NLV)

99. This is what happened: Sin came into the world by one man, **Adam**. Sin brought death with it. Death spread to all men because all have sinned. (Romans 5:12 NLV)

100. When **Haman** saw that Mordecai did not bow down or honor him, he was very angry. But he did not want to only hurt Mordecai. They had told him who the people of Mordecai were and Haman wanted to destroy all the Jews. He wanted to destroy all the people of Mordecai in the whole nation of Ahasuerus. (Esther 3:5–6 NLV)

HARD AS ROCK ANSWER KEY

1. **c) David**'s heart troubled him after he had numbered the people. So he said to the Lord, "I have sinned. But now I beg you, O Lord. Take away the sin of Your servant, for I have acted like a fool." (2 Samuel 24:10 NLV)

2. And **Samson** said, "With the jawbone of a donkey, heaps on heaps, with the jaw of a donkey I have slain a thousand men." (Judges 15:16 SKJV)

3. **False: Peter**. . .saw heaven open up and something like a large linen cloth being let down to earth by the four corners. On the cloth were all kinds of four-footed animals and snakes of the earth and birds of the sky. (Acts 10:9, 11–12 NLV)

4. **c) For the Sadducees** say that there is no resurrection, neither angel, nor spirit: but the Pharisees confess both. (Acts 23:8 KJV)

5. And **Jacob** went near unto Isaac his father; and he felt him, and said, The voice is Jacob's voice, but the hands are the hands of Esau. And he discerned him not, because his hands were hairy, as his brother Esau's hands: so he blessed him. (Genesis 27:22–23 KJV)

6. **c)** I am asking you for my son, **Onesimus**. He has become my son in the Christian life while I have been here in prison. (Philemon 10 NLV)

7. **a) Nathanael** said to Jesus, "How do You know me?" Jesus answered him, "Before Philip talked to you, I saw you under the fig tree." (John 1:48 NLV)

8. When he told about the special box of God, **Eli** fell back off the seat by the gate. His neck was broken and he died, for he was old and heavy. (1 Samuel 4:18 NLV)

9. **b)** Then Simon Peter, having a sword, drew it and struck the high priest's servant, and cut off his right ear. The servant's name was **Malchus**. (John 18:10 SKJV)

10. **True:** But the children of Israel committed a trespass in the accursed thing: for **Achan**. . .took of the accursed thing. (Joshua 7:1 KJV)

11. And he wrote in the letter, saying, "Station **Uriah** in the forefront of the fiercest position of battle and fall back from him, that he may be struck and die." (2 Samuel 11:15 SKJV)

12. **False:** Then one of the seraphim flew to me, with a burning coal which he had taken from the altar using a special tool. He touched my mouth with it. (**Isaiah** 6:6–7 NLV)

13. **c) Paul** spoke with strong words, "Sirs, it looks to me as if this ship and its freight will be lost." . . . The ship hit a place where the water was low. . . . The front of the ship did not move but the back part broke in pieces by the high waves. (Acts 27:9–10, 41 NLV)

14. And Nadab and **Abihu**, the sons of Aaron, took either of them his censer, and put fire therein, and put incense thereon, and offered strange fire before the LORD, which he commanded them not. (Leviticus 10:1 KJV)

15. **True:** But other of the apostles saw I none, save **James** the Lord's brother. (Galatians 1:19 KJV)

16. **d)** And they stoned **Stephen**, calling upon God, and saying, Lord Jesus, receive my spirit. (Acts 7:59 KJV)

17. Then one of His disciples, **Judas Iscariot**. . .said, "Why was this ointment not sold for three hundred pence and given to the poor?" He said this, not that he cared for the poor, but because he was a thief. (John 12:4–6 SKJV)

18. **False:** As they were on the way, they came to a man called **Simon from the country of Cyrene**. They made him carry the cross for Jesus. (Matthew 27:32 NLV)

19. And **Miriam** the prophetess, the sister of Aaron, took a timbrel in her hand, and all the women went out after her with timbrels and with dances. (Exodus 15:20 SKJV)

20. **a)** And while I was still praying, the man **Gabriel**. . .flew to me in a hurry. . . . He talked to me and told me things, saying, "O Daniel, I have now come to give you wisdom and understanding." (Daniel 9:21–22 NLV)

21. **True:** So **Naaman** came with his horses and with his chariot, and stood at the door of the house of Elisha. And Elisha sent a messenger unto him, saying, Go and wash in Jordan seven times, and thy flesh shall come again to thee, and thou shalt be clean. (2 Kings 5:9–10 KJV)

22. Paul and those with him went by ship from Paphos to the city of Perga in the country of Pamphylia. John **Mark** did not go with them but went back to Jerusalem. (Acts 13:13 NLV)

23. **False:** Some people brought a blind man

to **Jesus**. They asked if He would touch him. He took the blind man by the hand out of town. Then He spit on the eyes of the blind man and put His hands on him. (Mark 8:22–23 NLV)

24. **a)** And behold, **a man of Ethiopia, a eunuch**. . .was returning and sitting in his chariot reading Isaiah the prophet. Then the Spirit said to Philip, "Go near and join yourself to this chariot." And Philip ran to him. (Acts 8:27–30 SKJV)

25. **False:** In the selfsame day entered Noah, and Shem, and Ham, and Japheth, **the sons of Noah**, and Noah's wife, **and the three wives of his sons** with them, into the ark. (Genesis 7:13 KJV)

26. **False: Moses and Elijah** were seen talking to Jesus. (Matthew 17:3 NLV)

27. **b)** And when [Moses' mother] could not longer hide him, she took for him an ark of bulrushes, and daubed it with slime and with pitch, and put the child therein; and she laid it in the flags by the river's brink. And **his sister** stood afar off, to wit what would be done to him. (Exodus 2:3–4 KJV)

28. Heber's wife **Jael** took a big tent nail in her hand and a tool to hit it with. Because Sisera was very tired, he went into a deep sleep. She went to him in secret and hit the big nail into the side of his head. It went through and into the ground. So he died. (Judges 4:21 NLV)

29. **d)** So they threw **Jezebel** down. Some of her blood went on the wall and on the horses. . . . So they went to bury her. But all they found were her skull and feet and hands. (2 Kings 9:33, 35 NLV)

30. And Naomi said, Turn again, my daughters: why will ye go with me? . . . **Orpah** kissed her mother in law; but Ruth clave unto her. (Ruth 1:11, 14 KJV)

31. **a)** In the twentieth year of **Artaxerxes the king**. . .the king said to me, "Why is your face sad, since you are not sick? This is nothing but sorrow of heart." (Nehemiah 2:1–2 SKJV)

32. Then the woman said, "Whom should I bring up for you?" And he said, "Bring up **Samuel** for me." (1 Samuel 28:11 NLV)

33. **c)** And **Reuben** heard it, and he delivered him out of their hands; and said, Let us not kill him. (Genesis 37:21 KJV)

34. The dragon was thrown down to earth from heaven. This animal is the old snake. He is also called the Devil or **Satan**. (Revelation 12:9 NLV)

35. a) While **Pilate** was sitting in the place where he judges, **his wife** sent him this word, "Have nothing to do with that good Man. I have been troubled today in a dream about Him." (Matthew 27:19 NLV)

36. True: There came down from Judaea a certain prophet, named **Agabus.** And when he was come unto us, he took Paul's girdle, and bound his own hands and feet, and said, Thus saith the Holy Ghost, So shall the Jews at Jerusalem bind the man that owneth this girdle, and shall deliver him into the hands of the Gentiles. (Acts 21:10–11 KJV)

37. True: When Jesus saw Simon, He said, "You are Simon, the son of John. Your name will be Cephas." The name Cephas means **Peter**, or a rock. (John 1:42 NLV)

38. a) And **Samson** went and caught three hundred foxes and tied them tail to tail, and took firebrands and put a torch in the midst between two tails. . . . He let them go into the standing grain of the Philistines. (Judges 15:4–5 SKJV)

39. So **Ruth** went and gathered in the field behind those who picked the grain. (Ruth 2:3 NLV)

40. **True:** He brought the taxes to **Eglon king of Moab**. Now Eglon was a very fat man. . . . The whole sword went into his stomach and the fat closed over it. For he did not pull the sword out of his stomach. The insides of Eglon's stomach ran out. . . . They found their owner lying dead on the floor. (Judges 3:17, 22, 25 NLV)

41. **a) Jacob** went out from Beersheba, and went toward Haran. And he lighted upon a certain place, and tarried there all night, because the sun was set; and he took of the stones of that place, and put them for his pillows, and lay down in that place to sleep. (Genesis 28:10–11 KJV)

42. And **Barak** said to her, "If you will go with me, then I will go, but if you will not go with me, then I will not go." . . . And Deborah arose and went with Barak to Kedesh. (Judges 4:8–9 SKJV)

43. **b) King Belshazzar** gave a special supper for a thousand of his important men. . . . All at once the fingers of a man's hand were seen writing on the wall near the lamp-stand of the king's house. And the king saw the back of the hand as it wrote. (Daniel 5:1, 5 NLV)

44. Now Moses kept the flock of **Jethro** his father-in-law, the priest of Midian. (Exodus 3:1 SKJV)

45. **b)** And **the LORD** spake unto Moses and Aaron in the land of Egypt saying. . . I will pass through the land of Egypt this night, and will smite all the firstborn in the land of Egypt. (Exodus 12:1, 12 KJV)

46. **True: Hezekiah** answered, It is a light thing for the shadow to go down ten degrees: nay, but let the shadow return backward ten degrees. (2 Kings 20:10 KJV)

47. And when they arose early on the next morning, behold, **Dagon** had fallen on his face to the ground before the ark of the LORD. And the head of Dagon and both the palms of his hands were cut off on the threshold; only the stump of Dagon was left to him. (1 Samuel 5:4 SKJV)

48. **a)** But he hanged the chief **baker**: as Joseph had interpreted to them. (Genesis 40:22 KJV)

49. **False:** This letter is from **Paul**, a servant owned by God, and a missionary of Jesus Christ. (Titus 1:1 NLV)

50. **Jephthah** made a promise to the Lord and said, "You give the people of Ammon into my hand. And I will give to the Lord whatever comes out of the doors of my house to meet me when I return in peace from the people of Ammon. I will give it to the Lord as a burnt gift." (Judges 11:30–31 NLV)

51. **d)** When the morning came, Jacob saw that it was Leah. He said to **Laban**, "What have you done to me? Did I not work for you for Rachel? Why have you fooled me?" (Genesis 29:25 NLV)

52. **False:** In the fourth year of **Solomon**'s reign over Israel, in the month Zif, which is the second month, that he began to build the house of the LORD. (1 Kings 6:1 KJV)

53. "**Judah** is a lion's cub. From the prey, my son, you have gone up. He stooped down; he crouched as a lion, and as an old lion, who shall rouse him up?" (Genesis 49:9 SKJV)

54. **True:** Then **Noah** became a farmer and planted a grape-field. And he drank of the wine, and drank too much, and lay without covering himself in his tent. (Genesis 9:20–21 NLV)

55. And they gave forth their lots, and the lot

fell on **Matthias**. And he was numbered with the eleven apostles. (Acts 1:26 SKJV)

56. **a)** And he searched, and began at the eldest, and left at the youngest: and the cup was found in **Benjamin**'s sack.
(Genesis 44:12 KJV)

57. **True:** We met a servant-girl who could tell what was going to happen in the future by a demon she had. . . . She followed **Paul** and us crying out, "These are servants of the Highest God." (Acts 16:16–17 NLV)

58. **c) The Philistines** took the ark of God and brought it from Ebenezer to Ashdod.
(1 Samuel 5:1 SKJV)

59. But a certain man happened to shoot an arrow and hit the king of Israel between the parts of his battle-clothes. So **Ahab** said to the driver of his war-wagon, "Turn around and take me out of the battle. For I am hurt." The battle was hard that day, and the king was set up in his war-wagon in front of the Syrians. At evening he died.
(1 Kings 22:34–35 NLV)

60. **False:** And it came to pass, that in the morning watch the LORD looked unto the host of the Egyptians through the pillar of

fire and of the cloud, and troubled the host of the **Egyptians**, and took off their chariot wheels. (Exodus 14:24–25 KJV)

61. **d) Jesus** said, "Then their own people do not pay taxes. But so we will not make them to be troubled, go down to the lake and throw in a hook. Take the first fish that comes up. In its mouth you will find a piece of money." (Matthew 17:26–27 NLV)

62. When the Lord first spoke through **Hosea**, the Lord said to him, "Go and marry a wife who is not faithful in marriage, and have children from that woman. For the land is guilty of not being faithful to the Lord." (Hosea 1:2 NLV)

63. **False:** "Go and tell My servant **David**, 'This is what the Lord says, "Are you the one who should build a house for Me to live in?"''" (2 Samuel 7:5 NLV)

64. **c)** The words of **the Preacher**, the son of David, king in Jerusalem. (Ecclesiastes 1:1 KJV)

65. **a)** And the **angel** which I saw stand upon the sea and upon the earth lifted up his hand to heaven. (Revelation 10:5 KJV)

66. And upon a set day **Herod**, arrayed in royal apparel, sat upon his throne, and made an oration unto them. And the people gave a shout, saying, It is the voice of a god, and not of a man. And immediately the angel of the Lord smote him, because he gave not God the glory: and he was eaten of worms, and gave up the ghost. (Acts 12:21–23 KJV)

67. **True:** After they threw stones at him, they dragged him out of the city thinking he was dead. As the Christians gathered around **Paul**, he got up and went back into the city. (Acts 14:19–20 NLV)

68. **c)** "Why did you allow your heart to do this? You have lied to God, not to men." When **Ananias** heard these words, he fell down dead. (Acts 5:4–5 NLV)

69. "But I say to you that **Elijah** has already come, and they did not know him but have done to him whatever they wished." . . . Then the disciples understood that He spoke to them of John the Baptist. (Matthew 17:12–13 SKJV)

70. **False: David** sat between the two gates. . . . And the king was very moved and went up to the chamber over the gate and wept.

And as he went, he said this, "O my son Absalom, my son, my son Absalom! I wish I had died instead of you, O Absalom, my son, my son!" (2 Samuel 18:24, 33 SKJV)

71. **d) Moses** said, "I pray to You, show me Your shining-greatness!" And God said. . . "I will cover you with My hand until I have passed by. Then I will take My hand away and you will see My back." (Exodus 33:18–19, 22–23 NLV)

72. **False:** When Jesus was born in Bethlehem of Judaea in the days of Herod the king, behold, there came **wise men** from the east to Jerusalem. . . . And when they were come into the house. . .they presented unto him gifts; gold, and frankincense and myrrh. (Matthew 2:1, 11 KJV)

73. **Melchizedek** king of Salem brought forth bread and wine: and he was the priest of the most high God. And he blessed him, and said, Blessed be Abram of the most high God. . .possessor of heaven and earth. (Genesis 14:18–19 KJV)

74. **a)** And it came to pass, as she continued praying before the LORD, that Eli marked her mouth. Now **Hannah**, she spake in her

heart; only her lips moved, but her voice was not heard: therefore Eli thought she had been drunken. (1 Samuel 1:12–13 KJV)

75. Then **Jonah** prayed to the Lord his God while in the stomach of the fish, saying. . . "Waters closed in over me. The sea was all around me. Weeds were around my head." (Jonah 2:1–2, 5 NLV)

76. **c)** For the prophecy did not come in old time by the will of man, but holy men of God spoke as they were moved by the **Holy Spirit**. (2 Peter 1:21 SKJV)

77. True: "Vanity of vanities," says **the Preacher**. "Vanity of vanities; all is vanity." (Ecclesiastes 1:2 SKJV)

78. For I was the king's cupbearer. (**Nehemiah** 1:11 SKJV)

79. **a)** And the LORD said unto Cain, Where is **Abel** thy brother? And he said, I know not: Am I my brother's keeper? And he said, What hast thou done? the voice of thy brother's blood crieth unto me from the ground. (Genesis 4:9–10 KJV)

80. True: **Samson** tore the lion apart like one tears a young goat. . . . He saw that a lot of bees and some honey were inside the lion's body. So he took the honey out with his hands and went on his way, eating as he went. (Judges 14:6, 8–9 NLV)

81. **c)** I, **John**, who also am your brother and companion in tribulation and in the kingdom and patience of Jesus Christ, was in the isle that is called Patmos for the word of God and for the testimony of Jesus Christ. (Revelation 1:9 SKJV)

82. And before I had done speaking in mine heart, behold, **Rebekah** came forth with her pitcher on her shoulder. . .and said, Drink, and I will give thy camels drink also: so I drank, and she made the camels drink also. (Genesis 24:45–46 KJV)

83. **True:** Now **Joseph** was strong and good-looking. The time came when his boss's wife saw him, and she said, "Lie with me." But he would not do it. (Genesis 39:6–8 NLV)

84. **b)** Some young boys came out from the city and made fun of him. They said to him, "Go up, you man with no hair! Go up, you man with no hair!" . . . **Elisha** went from there to Mount Carmel, then returned to Samaria. (2 Kings 2:23, 25 NLV)

85. Then **Peter** said to Jesus, "Lord, it is good for us to be here. If You will let us, we will build three altars here. One will be for You and one for Moses and one for Elijah." (Matthew 17:4 NLV)

86. **a)** That night the **angel** of the Lord went out and killed 185,000 men among the Assyrian tents. When those left alive got up early in the morning, they saw all the dead bodies. (2 Kings 19:35 NLV)

87. Then **Herod**. . .sent them to Bethlehem and said, "Go and find the young Child. When you find Him, let me know. Then I can go and worship Him also." (Matthew 2:7–8 NLV)

88. **False:** When **John the Baptist** was in prison, he heard what Jesus was doing. He sent his followers. They asked, "Are You the One Who was to come, or should we look for another?" (Matthew 11:2–3 NLV)

89. **d)** Then **Abraham** looked and saw a ram behind him, with his horns caught in the bushes. Abraham went and took the ram, and gave him as a burnt gift instead of his son. (Genesis 22:13 NLV)

90. This letter is from **Paul**, a missionary for Jesus Christ. God wanted me to work for Him. (Colossians 1:1 NLV)

91. **a)** When Boaz had finished eating and drinking and his heart was happy, he went to lie down beside the grain. Then **Ruth** came in secret. She took the covers off his feet and lay down. (Ruth 3:7 NLV)

92. Now **Moses** was a man with no pride, more so than any man on the earth. (Numbers 12:3 NLV)

93. **c)** Then the name of **Saul** the son of Kish was drawn. But when they looked for him, he could not be found. So they asked the Lord, "Has the man come here yet?" The Lord said, "See, he is hiding among the bags." (1 Samuel 10:21–22 NLV)

94. **False:** Then Jerubbaal, who is **Gideon**, and all the people that were with him, rose up early, and pitched beside the well of Harod. (Judges 7:1 KJV)

95. **a)** Three days later there was a wedding in the town of Cana in the country of Galilee. **The mother of Jesus** was there. Jesus and His followers were asked to come to the wedding. (John 2:1–2 NLV)

96. **False:** The **sons of God** saw that the daughters of men were beautiful. And they took wives for themselves, whomever they chose. (Genesis 6:2 NLV)

97. How art thou fallen from heaven, O **Lucifer**, son of the morning! . . . For thou hast said in thine heart. . .I will be like the most High. Yet thou shalt be brought down to hell, to the sides of the pit. (Isaiah 14:12–15 KJV)

98. **a)** And one of the elders saith unto me, Weep not: behold, **the Lion of the tribe of Judah**, the Root of David, hath prevailed to open the book, and to loose the seven seals thereof. (Revelation 5:5 KJV)

99. And I will give power unto my two **witnesses**, and they shall prophesy a thousand two hundred and threescore days, clothed in sackcloth. . . . And if any man will hurt them, fire proceedeth out of their mouth, and devoureth their enemies. (Revelation 11:3, 5 KJV)

100. **False:** After some days the Jews talked together and made plans how they might kill **Saul**. . . . So the followers helped him get away at night. They let him down **over the wall in a basket.** (Acts 9:23, 25 NLV)

WE HOPE YOU'RE A GOOD
GUESSER ANSWER KEY

1. And it came to pass, that on the morrow Moses went into the tabernacle of witness; and, behold, the rod of **Aaron** for the house of Levi was budded, and brought forth buds, and bloomed blossoms, and yielded almonds. (Numbers 17:8 KJV)

2. **a)** But the prince of the kingdom of Persia withstood me one and twenty days: but, lo, **Michael**, one of the chief princes, came to help me. (Daniel 10:13 KJV)

3. The earth opened its mouth and took them and all those of their house, and all **Korah**'s men and all that belonged to them. (Numbers 16:32 NLV)

4. **c)** One of the women who listened sold purple cloth. She was from the city of Thyatira. Her name was **Lydia** and she was a worshiper of God. The Lord opened her heart to hear what Paul said. (Acts 16:14 NLV)

5. **True:** "Also take for yourself wheat and barley and beans and lentils and millet and spelt, and put them in one container, and make bread from it for yourself." (**Ezekiel** 4:9 SKJV)

6. **c)** And the ark of the LORD continued in the house of **Obededom** the Gittite three months: and the LORD blessed Obededom, and all his household. (2 Samuel 6:11 KJV)

7. **False:** I remember your true faith. It is the same faith your grandmother **Lois** had and your mother Eunice had. I am sure you have that same faith also. (2 Timothy 1:5 NLV)

8. So **Mephibosheth** dwelt in Jerusalem: for he did eat continually at the king's table; and was lame on both his feet. (2 Samuel 9:13 KJV)

9. A man named **Demetrius** made small silver buildings for the worship of Diana. His workmen received much money for their work. (Acts 19:24 NLV)

10. **b)** He took Elijah's coat that fell from him, and hit the water and said, "Where is the Lord, the God of Elijah?" When he hit the water, it was divided to one side and to the other, and **Elisha** crossed the Jordan. (2 Kings 2:14 NLV)

11. **True:** For it was so, when Jezebel cut off the prophets of the LORD, that **Obadiah** took an hundred prophets, and hid them by fifty in a cave, and fed them with bread and water. (1 Kings 18:4 KJV)

12. **c) Barnabas** wanted to take John Mark with them. Paul did not think it was good to take him because he had left them while they were in Pamphylia. He had not helped them in the work. (Acts 15:37–38 NLV)

13. This letter is from **Paul**. . . . See what big letters I make when I write to you with my own hand. (Galatians 1:1; 6:11 NLV)

14. **c)** When any of the **Ephraimite** men ran away and said, "Let me cross over," the men of Gilead would say to him, "Are you an Ephraimite?" If he said, "No," they would say to him, "Then say 'Shibboleth.'" But he would say, "Sibboleth," for he could not say it right. So they would take hold of him and kill him at the crossing places of the Jordan. (Judges 12:5–6 NLV)

15. And the watchman told, saying, He came even unto them, and cometh not again: and the driving is like the driving of **Jehu** the son of Nimshi; for he driveth furiously. (2 Kings 9:20 KJV)

16. **d)** And after three months we departed in a ship of Alexandria that had wintered in the isle, whose sign was **Castor and Pollux**. (Acts 28:11 SKJV)

17. **False:** And David said to **Abigail**, Blessed be the LORD God of Israel, which sent thee this day to meet me: And blessed be thy advice, and blessed be thou, which hast kept me this day from. . .avenging myself with mine own hand. (1 Samuel 25:32–33 KJV)

18. **c)** These are the words of **Amos**, a shepherd of Tekoa, which he received in special dreams about Israel two years before the earth shook. (Amos 1:1 NLV)

19. **Elisha** said to her, "What can I do for you?" . . . And she said, "Your woman servant has nothing in the house except a jar of oil." Then he said, "Go around and get jars from all your neighbors. Get empty jars, many of them. Then go in and shut the door behind you and your sons. Pour the oil into all these jars, and set aside each one that is full." (2 Kings 4:2–4 NLV)

20. **True:** And as the ark of the LORD came into the city of David, **Michal** Saul's daughter looked through a window, and saw king David leaping and dancing before the LORD; and she despised him in her heart. (2 Samuel 6:16 KJV)

21. **False:** But **Jonathan** heard not when his father charged the people with the oath: wherefore he put forth the end of the rod that was in his hand, and dipped it in an honeycomb, and put his hand to his mouth. (1 Samuel 14:27 KJV)

22. The king's head ruler gave them new names. To **Daniel** he gave the name Belteshazzar. (Daniel 1:7 NLV)

23. **a)** That day Pilate and **Herod** became friends. Before that they had worked against each other. (Luke 23:12 NLV)

24. **Ham,** the father of Canaan, saw the nakedness of his father and told his two brothers outside. . . . And Noah awoke from his wine and knew what his younger son had done to him. And he said, "Cursed be Canaan." (Genesis 9:22, 24–25 SKJV)

25. **False:** So Lot went out to speak to his sons-in-law who were to marry his daughters. He said, "Get up! Get out of this place! For the Lord will destroy the city!" But **his sons-in-law** thought he was only joking. (Genesis 19:14 NLV)

26. **b)** It seemed good to me also, having had perfect understanding of all things from

the very first, to write to you in order, most excellent **Theophilus**. (Luke 1:3 SKJV)

27. She said to them, "Do not call me **Naomi**. Call me Mara. For the All-powerful has brought much trouble to me." (Ruth 1:20 NLV)

28. **False:** But Amasa took no heed to the sword that was in Joab's hand: so he smote him therewith **in the fifth rib**, and shed out his bowels to the ground, and struck him not again; and he died. (2 Samuel 20:10 KJV)

29. a) **A young man** was following Him with only a piece of cloth around his body. They put their hands on the young man. Leaving the cloth behind, he ran away with no clothes on. (Mark 14:51–52 NLV)

30. And one of them named **Agabus** stood up and signified by the Spirit that there would be great famine throughout all the world, which came to pass in the days of Claudius Caesar. (Acts 11:28 SKJV)

31. **False:** We entered into the house of Philip the evangelist, who was one of the seven, and abided with him. And the same man had **four** daughters, virgins, who prophesied. (Acts 21:8–9 SKJV)

32. But when **Peter** came to Antioch, I had to stand up against him because he was guilty. (Galatians 2:11 NLV)

33. **b) The people of Gibeon** heard what Joshua had done to Jericho and Ai. So they went out to fool him, as men from another land. They took old bags on their donkeys, and skin bags of wine that were old and torn and mended. They wore old and mended shoes on their feet, and old clothes on themselves. All their bread was dry and broken. (Joshua 9:3–5 NLV)

34. **False:** And she named the child **Ichabod**, saying, The glory is departed from Israel. (1 Samuel 4:21 KJV)

35. **b)** And Moses was content to dwell with the man, and he gave Moses his daughter **Zipporah**. (Exodus 2:21 SKJV)

36. The elder unto the elect lady and her children. (2 **John** 1 KJV)

37. **False: Absalom**'s hair caught in the branches of the oak. . . . Then Joab. . .took three spears in his hand and threw them through Absalom's heart while he was still alive in the oak. (2 Samuel 18:9, 14 NLV)

38. And on the next day, when Agrippa and **Bernice** had come with great pomp and had entered into the place of hearing with the chief captains and principal men of the city, Paul was brought forth at Festus's commandment. (Acts 25:23 SKJV)

39. **a) Ehud** put out his left hand, took the sword from his right leg, and pushed it into Eglon's stomach. (Judges 3:21 NLV)

40. **False:** "A traveler came to **the rich man**. And he refrained from taking of his own flock and of his own herd to prepare for the traveler who had come to him, but he took the poor man's lamb and prepared it for the man who had come to him." (2 Samuel 12:4 SKJV)

41. David therefore sent out spies, and understood that **Saul** was come in very deed. . . . Then said Abishai to David, God hath delivered thine enemy into thine hand this day: now therefore let me smite him, I pray thee, with the spear even to the earth at once, and I will not smite him the second time. (1 Samuel 26:4, 8 KJV)

42. **c)** For only **Og** king of Bashan was left of the children of the Rephaim. His bed was made of iron. It is in Rabbah of the sons of Ammon. It was as long as five steps, and as wide as two long steps. (Deuteronomy 3:11 NLV)

43. **True:** But it came to pass in the morning, when the wine had gone out of Nabal, and his wife had told him these things, that his heart died within him, and he became as a stone. And it came to pass, after about ten days, that the LORD struck **Nabal** so that he died. (1 Samuel 25:37–38 SKJV)

44. **c)** And he said, Go up, say unto Ahab, Prepare thy chariot, and get thee down that the rain stop thee not. . . . And the hand of the LORD was on Elijah; and he girded up his loins, and ran before **Ahab** to the entrance of Jezreel. (1 Kings 18:44, 46 KJV)

45. **c)** And it shall come to pass afterward, that I will pour out my spirit upon all flesh; and your sons and your daughters shall prophesy, your old men shall dream dreams, your young men shall see visions. (**Joel** 2:28 KJV)

46. And **Deborah**, a prophetess, the wife of Lapidoth. . .dwelled under the palm tree of Deborah between Ramah and Bethel in the mountains of Ephraim. (Judges 4:4–5 SKJV)

47. **True:** And when king David came to Bahurim, behold, thence came out a man of the family of the house of Saul, whose name was **Shimei**, the son of Gera: he came forth, and cursed still as he came. (2 Samuel 16:5 KJV)

48. **a) Shem** and Japheth took a garment, and laid it upon both their shoulders, and went backward, and covered the nakedness of their father; and their faces were backward, and they saw not their father's nakedness. (Genesis 9:23 KJV)

49. Amram married his father's sister **Jochebed**. She gave birth to his sons, Aaron and Moses. (Exodus 6:20 NLV)

50. **False: Hiram** gave Solomon as much as he wanted of the cedar and cypress trees. (1 Kings 5:10 NLV)

51. **c)** And they slew the sons of **Zedekiah** before his eyes, and put out the eyes of Zedekiah, and bound him with bronze shackles, and carried him to Babylon. (2 Kings 25:7 SKJV)

52. And King **Rehoboam** consulted with the old men who stood before his father. . . . But he ignored the counsel that the old men had given him and consulted with the young men who had grown up with him. (1 Kings 12:6, 8 SKJV)

53. **c)** They brought two men in front of them. They were **Joseph**, also called Barsabbas Justus, and Matthias. . . . Then they drew names and the name of Matthias was chosen. (Acts 1:23, 26 NLV)

54. Now these are the generations of Terah: Terah begot Abram, Nahor, and Haran, and **Haran** begot Lot. (Genesis 11:27 SKJV)

55. **False: John's followers** heard this. They went and took his body and buried it. (Mark 6:29 NLV)

56. **c) Elisha** prayed and said, "O Lord, I pray, open his eyes, that he may see." And the Lord opened the servant's eyes, and he saw. He saw that the mountain was full of horses and war-wagons of fire all around Elisha. (2 Kings 6:17 NLV)

57. So Sennacherib king of **Assyria** departed. . . . And it came to pass, as he was worshipping in the house of Nisroch his god, that Adrammelech and Sharezer his sons smote him with the sword. (Isaiah 37:37–38 KJV)

58. **True:** And this whole land shall be a desolation and an astonishment, and these nations shall serve the king of Babylon seventy years. (**Jeremiah** 25:11 SKJV)

59. **c)** [David] changed the way he acted in front of them. He pretended to be crazy while he was with them. He made marks on the doors of the gate. He let his spit run down into the hair of his face. Then **Achish** said to his servants, "See, you see the man is crazy." (1 Samuel 21:13–14 NLV)

60. When the Lord first spoke through Hosea, the Lord said to him, "Go and marry a wife who is not faithful in marriage." . . . So he married **Gomer** the daughter of Diblaim and she gave birth to his son. (Hosea 1:2–3 NLV)

61. **False:** And when he thus had spoken, he cried with a loud voice, Lazarus, come forth. And he that was dead came forth, bound hand and foot with graveclothes: and his face was bound about with a napkin. (**John** 11:43–44 KJV)

62. **a)** This letter is from Paul. . . . I was born a Jew and came from the family group of **Benjamin**. (Philippians 1:1; 3:5 NLV)

63. Now **Elihu** had waited till Job had spoken, because they were elder than he. When Elihu saw that there was no answer in the mouth of these three men, then his wrath was kindled. (Job 32:4–5 KJV)

64. **d)** Unto whom the prince of the eunuchs gave names: for he gave unto Daniel the name of Belteshazzar; and to Hananiah, of Shadrach; and to Mishael, of Meshach; and to Azariah, of **Abednego**. (Daniel 1:7 KJV)

65. **False:** And when the man was let down, and touched the bones of **Elisha**, he revived, and stood up on his feet. (2 Kings 13:21 KJV)

66. They brought the sick people and laid them on the streets hoping that if **Peter** walked by, his shadow would fall on some of them. (Acts 5:15 NLV)

67. **d)** Then the Word of the Lord came to me a second time, saying, "Take the belt that you have bought and are wearing, get up, and go to the Euphrates. Hide it there in a hole in the rock." (**Jeremiah** 13:3–4 NLV)

68. The **cherubim** shall stretch out their wings on high, covering the mercy seat with their wings, and their faces shall look to one another. (Exodus 25:20 SKJV)

69. **True:** When **Esau** was forty years old, he married Judith the daughter of Beeri the Hittite, and Basemath the daughter of Elon the Hittite. And they made life full of sorrow for Isaac and Rebekah. (Genesis 26:34–35 NLV)

70. **b)** The words of King **Lemuel**, the prophecy that his mother taught him. (Proverbs 31:1 SKJV)

71. **Michael** was one of the head angels. He argued with the devil about the body of Moses. But Michael would not speak sharp words to the devil, saying he was guilty. He said, "The Lord speaks sharp words to you." (Jude 9 NLV)

72. **False:** "Do not make the whole army fight, for **the people of Ai** are few." So about 3,000 men of Israel went, but they ran away from the men of Ai. (Joshua 7:3–4 NLV)

73. **b)** O foolish **Galatians**, who hath bewitched you, that ye should not obey the truth, before whose eyes Jesus Christ hath been evidently set forth, crucified among you? (Galatians 3:1 KJV)

74. "Your sons and your daughters were eating and drinking wine in their eldest brother's house. And, behold, a great wind came from the wilderness and struck the four corners of the house. And it fell on the young men, and they are dead." . . . Then **Job** arose and tore his robe and shaved his head. (Job 1:18–20 SKJV)

75. d) "For as **Jonah** was three days and three nights in the whale's belly, so shall the Son of Man be three days and three nights in the heart of the earth." (Matthew 12:40 SKJV)

76. I, **John**. . .was in the Spirit on the Lord's Day, and heard behind me a great voice, as of a trumpet. (Revelation 1:9–10 SKJV)

77. **True:** In those days I also saw Jews who had married wives of Ashdod, of Ammon, and of Moab. . . . And I contended with them, and cursed them, and struck some of them, and plucked out their hair. (**Nehemiah** 13:23, 25 SKJV)

78. b) King Ahasuerus. . .wanted to show her beauty to the people and the princes, for she was beautiful. But Queen **Vashti** would not come when the king sent his servants to bring her. So the king became very angry

and his anger burned within him.
(Esther 1:10–12 NLV)

79. Afterward he measured a thousand, and it was a river that I could not cross over, for the waters had risen—waters to swim in, a river that could not be crossed over. (**Ezekiel** 47:5 SKJV)

80. **False:** And I stood upon the sand of the sea, and saw a **beast** rise up out of the sea, having seven heads and ten horns. (Revelation 13:1 KJV)

81. **c)** So all who fell from **Benjamin** that day were twenty-five thousand men who drew the sword. All these were men of valor. But six hundred men turned and fled to the wilderness to the rock of Rimmon. (Judges 20:46–47 SKJV)

82. Then **Jehu** gathered all the people and said to them, "Ahab worshiped Baal a little. Jehu will worship him much." . . . But Jehu did this to fool them, so that he might destroy the worshipers of Baal. (2 Kings 10:18–19 NLV)

83. **b)** And the man **Micah** had a house of gods. . . . Then Micah said, "Now I know that the LORD will do good for me, since I have a Levite as my priest." (Judges 17:5, 13 SKJV)

84. **True:** Some women who had been healed of demons and diseases were with Him. **Mary Magdalene**, who had had seven demons put out of her, was one of them. (Luke 8:2 NLV)

85. **Jesus** answered and said unto them. . . . Woe unto thee, Chorazin! woe unto thee, Bethsaida! (Matthew 11:4, 21 KJV)

86. c) And after six days Jesus taketh **Peter, James, and John** his brother, and bringeth them up into an high mountain apart, and was transfigured before them. (Matthew 17:1–2 KJV)

87. Then **Paul** said to him, "God shall strike you, you whitewashed wall!" . . . And those who stood by said, "Do you revile God's high priest?" Then Paul said, "I did not know, brothers, that he was the high priest. (Acts 23:3–5 SKJV)

88. So the LORD blessed the latter end of Job. . . . He also had seven sons and three daughters. And he called the name of the first, Jemimah; and the name of the second, Keziah; and the name of the third, Keren-happuch. And in all the land no women were found so beautiful as the daughters of **Job**. (Job 42:12–15 SKJV)

89. c) Therefore they commanded **the children of Benjamin**, saying, "Go and lie in wait in the vineyards and watch. And behold, if the daughters of Shiloh come out to perform their dances, then you come out of the vineyards, and every man catch for himself his wife from the daughters of Shiloh." (Judges 21:20–21 SKJV)

90. And when Jesus was come into **Peter**'s house, he saw his wife's mother laid, and sick of a fever. And he touched her hand, and the fever left her: and she arose, and ministered unto them. (Matthew 8:14–15 KJV)

91. And when **Paul** wanted to enter in to the people, the disciples did not allow him. And some of the chiefs of Asia who were his friends sent to him, asking him not to venture into the theater. (Acts 19:30–31 SKJV)

92. d) This is the word about Nineveh, the book of the special dream of **Nahum** the Elkoshite. (Nahum 1:1 NLV)

93. **True:** Abimelech. . .killed his brothers, the sons of Jerubbaal. He killed all seventy men upon one stone. But Jerubbaal's **youngest son Jotham was left alive**, because he hid himself. (Judges 9:4–5 NLV)

94. At that time Merodach-baladan son of Baladan, king of Babylon, sent letters and a gift to Hezekiah. He heard that he had been sick and had become well. **Hezekiah** was pleased and showed them all his store-house of riches. (Isaiah 39:1–2 NLV)

95. **b)** Now **Rachel** had taken the gods of Laban's house and put them in the seat that was used on the camel's back. And she sat upon them. (Genesis 31:34 NLV)

96. **False:** But the names of the sons of Moses the man of God were among the family of Levi. The sons of **Moses** were Gershom and Eliezer. (1 Chronicles 23:14–15 NLV)

97. Then **Jacob** took green sticks of three kinds of trees. And he cut white marks in them, showing the white which was in the sticks. He took these sticks which he had cut and set them in front of the flocks, in the place where the flocks came to drink. (Genesis 30:37–38 NLV)

98. **c)** So they went and came to the house of **Rahab**. . . . The men said to her, "We will be free from this promise you have made us swear unless, when we come into the land, you tie this red rope in the window you let us down through." (Joshua 2:1, 17–18 NLV)

99. **False:** They got up early in the morning. The sun was shining on the water. And **the Moabites** saw that the water beside them was as red as blood. They said, "This is blood. For sure the kings have fought and killed one another." (2 Kings 3:22–23 NLV)

100. **d)** That very night Belshazzar the king of Babylon was killed. So **Darius the Mede** became the king when he was sixty-two years old. (Daniel 5:30–31 NLV)

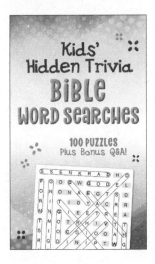